CLASS ACTS

CLASS ACTS

Etiquette for Today

Eve Drobot

VNR VAN NOSTRAND REINHOLD COMPANY
NEW YORK CINCINNATI TORONTO LONDON MELBORNE

ACKNOWLEDGMENTS

As I am a great believer in thank-yous, it would only be fitting to extend my gratitude to the people who were instrumental in making this book happen:

Stephanie Cox and Lesley Mang, who conceived it;
Nancy Colbert, Laurie Coulter, Valerie Wyatt and
Barbara Ravage, who midwifed it;
and Brian Segal, who baptized it.

I would also like to thank Sheba for having such a deliciously complicated life;

and Jack, without whom 99 44/100s percent of most things would be impossible.

Published in the United States in 1982
by Van Nostrand Reinhold Company Inc.
135 West 50th Street
New York, NY 10020, U.S.A.

Library of Congress
Catalog Card Number 82-4831

Printed and bound in the United States of America

16 15 14 13 12 11 10 9 8 7 6 5 4 3 2 1

Library of Congress Cataloging in Publication Data

Drobot, Eve.
Class acts: etiquette for today.

Includes index.
1. Etiquette. I. Title.

BJ1853.D66 395 82-4831
ISBN 0-442-29663-0 AACR2

To my parents, Wanda and Jan,
for having brought me up so well

CONTENTS

Introduction

Who needs a book of etiquette?

"Who needs a book of etiquette?" asked Amy Vanderbilt in the preface to the 1952 edition of her *Complete Book* of same. "Everyone," was the succinct answer. Today "everyone" includes not only the about-to-be-marrieds, who have traditionally turned to the encyclopedists of decorum in their anxiety to Do It Right, but also the about-to-be-unmarrieds who, until now, have had nowhere to turn. And why shouldn't there be a protocol of parting? If there are psychiatrists to keep your head together and lawyers to keep your property apart, why not someone to suggest a gracious way to say good-bye?

I hung out my shingle as a social arbiter shortly after I had read an article in one of the weekend supplements about the sorry state of social graces among men and women who found themselves suddenly single. "The real source of anxiety for many unmarried people," said one man, "is not knowing where they fit in. So they feel guilty and insecure. They need a new code of behavior, like an updated version of Emily Post's etiquette book, to replace the traditional rules that no longer apply to them."

The idea behind the column was simple: an uptown Ann Landers, willing to lend an ear to the trials and tribulations not of the God-fearing, middle-aged middle class, but of sophisticated young urbanites in pursuit of cool. I expected to be inundated with smart-ass queries about outlandish situations, but to my surprise, the majority of my readers' letters were quite straightforward. Which fork and knife does one use? How much should I tip? What is proper to wear to a funeral? The questions I received made me realize that my generation is slipping into an age when we must deal with life's traditions — births, marriages, deaths and dinner parties — yet many of us don't have a clue about what is expected of us.

We have recently lived through twenty extremely rude years. The Sixties confused politeness with political repression and rebelled against it, while the Seventies (a.k.a. The Me Decade) violated the primary rule of good manners, which is simply to be considerate of others. It was all very well to live with complete disregard for propriety on a soybean farming commune in New Mexico or in a therapeutic group home north of Vancouver. But now we are thirty and then some. We have shucked our blue jeans in favor of three-piece suits; we are junior members of law firms, account executives for multinational corporations or presidents of our own film companies. We have to take clients out for lunch, attend cocktail parties and travel on business. Our friends are getting married in churches and synagogues instead of in hot air balloons over the Rockies, and we have to make small talk with grandmothers at their receptions. We are expected to attend christenings, organize anniversary parties for our parents, and RSVP to invitations for art gallery openings. *And we don't know how.*

This book is not meant to be the last word on Dos and Don'ts in polite society: few of us will ever need to worry about the correct way to address a Rear Admiral at a White House dinner. For the truly upscale occasions, where strict protocol is in force, I heartily recommend you refer to the more comprehensive works on the subject, such as the revised editions of Amy Vanderbilt and Emily Post. They are invaluable, and this book is not meant to be a substitute for them.

I take a slightly more skewed approach to manners. I hold with Lord Chesterfield, who defined manners as "trifles, little attentions, mere nothings [which] will make you liked or disliked." Some of the things we think of as "proper" are mere annoyances — edicts to Do This or Don't Do That which are the preserve of maiden aunts who have nothing better to do with their time but fuss. This sort of "etiquette" just gets in the way of life.

Let me give you an example. Every year in the spring, I quietly mark Who Cares What Color You Wear on Your Feet Week. It's a small celebration of living in an age when one is freed from observing silly rules. You may recall that once upon a time, not so very long ago, ladies simply did not, must not, could not and should not wear black shoes after Easter Sunday nor white shoes before. And vice versa on Labor Day. I was brought up to believe that if I did the ground would open up, the heavens would spew forth and, at the very least, my shoes would be ruined. This has never happened even though I have been brazenly sporting black sandals for several summers now. And I have lived to tell the tale, which only goes to prove that if enough people break a rule, it stops being one — a philosophy of etiquette I heartily espouse.

Most of the rules that have been broken in recent times simply had to go, thanks to women's liberation. Chapter Two deals specifically with some of the issues this long-called-for breakdown in tradition has created, but throughout I have functioned on the assumption that feminism is a Good Thing. Forget notions of chivalry based on the idea of women as frail little "things." But forget equally that *any* show of consideration toward a woman is an insult to her hard-won sense of equality. It would be wonderful indeed if we could get to the point where we could all be plain, old-fashioned nice to each other, regardless of sex.

It was in this spirit that I responded to the following query which, to my amazement, proved to be one of the burning questions of the day.

> ***DEAR EVE:*** *Who goes through a revolving door first — a man or a woman? R.R.*

> Whoever gets there first. This is where old-fashioned etiquette starts to get really silly. The hard-and-fast rule, before our enlightened times, was that the man went first because the poor dear could hardly be expected to have enough strength to get the damn thing rolling. Unless, of course, there was a doorman, in which case he gave it a shove and Madame went gliding through before M'sieur. Unless, of course, it was rush hour in which case, I suppose, the gentleman would body-check everyone else trying to get through and give the lady a fighting chance. What difference does it make? If you like each other enough, squeeze into one compartment together. Go around twice. You go first on Tuesdays and she goes first on Fridays. Next question, please.

CHAPTER ONE

Introductions

The Finer Points of

In social situations, a lot of you worry about who's who and what's what and rightly so. Proper introductions are the sine qua non of intercourse, social or otherwise, and making them is an art in danger of going the way of morning milk deliveries, parking in midtown Manhattan and helpful salespeople in the major department stores.

In our laid-back world, complete strangers have been known to go up to one another and begin conversations, but it wasn't all that long ago that this was just Not Done. Without a formal introduction, a lady and a gentleman were obliged to ignore each other, even though they might have remarked upon each other's existence on countless occasions in the street or at social events. In a society stable enough to afford the luxury of frowning on immediate intimacy, there was a logic to this: a third party was necessary to sanction any new relationship.

The deceptively simple declaration of fact, "Miss Bartholomew, this is Freddy MacHaggis the Fourth," was in fact a cleverly disguised tribal incantation which, to the trained ear, went something like this: "It's quite all right to be seen in public with this fellow. I've personally known him since the days of Miss MacTavish's dancing school, and our families crossed together on the *Mayflower*.

"Our parents belong to the same country club, and his second cousin is a member of my uncle's brokerage firm. He went to Choate, has a trust fund, is an excellent fourth for bridge and can be counted on to discuss the theater intelligently at the dinner table."

Without all this information, one wouldn't be caught dead striking up a conversation. Which is precisely the situation that Dorothy L. Sayers so rightly ridiculed in *The Unpleasantness at the Bellona Club*. An elderly member succumbs in his favorite armchair by the fire. Rigor mortis sets in, and no one notices for several hours because the older members are used to seeing him sitting there stiffly and the younger members have not been given the right to address him.

Times, thank heavens, do change, but the principle — it helps to know to whom one is speaking — remains the same. I've had my share, thank you very much, of shifting my feet on the sidewalk while my companion strikes up a conversation with a passing acquaintance he neglects to present to me, reasoning, no doubt, that he'll tie us up interminably if he doesn't keep the proceedings to a simple "Hi! What's new? Gotta dash — I'll give you a call."

Tsk, tsk, I say. No one should be made to feel as though he or she doesn't exist, and that is precisely what not introducing someone accomplishes. The person thus ignored is left with two options, both of them unpleasant. He or she can jump right in with a "Hi, I'm someone too" or wait until the third party has left to deliver a sermon on the etiquette of introductions. There's no easy way out. Don't ever put your friends in this position, that's all I ask.

It may be embarrassing to proffer an introduction only to be told, "Thanks, we've already met," but it's nowhere near as excruciating as spending an evening discussing the meaning of the universe with someone whose identity remains a total mystery. While we all still have names, not numbers, it pays to use them so we don't get out of practice.

DEAR EVE: *I have a friend who takes introductions to their extreme — or at least I think he does. When he has ten people or so over for an evening, he stops the proceedings every time a new person arrives to make (often long-winded) introductions. What do you advise for small gatherings? G.O'R.*

Unless your host has a butler stationed at the doorway to intone, "The Baron and Baroness von Twittentropp," he really should interrupt whatever proceedings are underway to introduce each newcomer to the assembled company. When he has gone through the litany of "MarySusanBobSandyLindaGordonLaurieJackand" — deep breath — "Peter" for the sixth time, you might think it's all pointless because who the hell is going to remember it anyway? But figure it like this: the earlier arrivals will have had enough choruses for most of the names to sink in, and the later arrivals will have the perfect excuse to say, as they settle into the chair next to someone who is still a stranger, "Larry went through the cast of characters so quickly, I didn't catch your name."

Big bashes are another case altogether, and no one in his right mind expects the host or hostess to spend most of a cocktail party endlessly making introductions. After all, they have as much right to sample the canapés as anyone else. If you're thinking of throwing such a bash, however, you should make a point of greeting each new arrival personally, making sure he or she is furnished with a drink and at least one name to start off the daisy chain. Pop into established groups occasionally with fresh blood in tow, but other than that, it's every guest for him or herself.

DEAR EVE: *I go to a lot of parties and spend a lot of time making small talk with people I'm not really interested in getting to know. Don't you think a host or hostess could cut a lot of corners for guests if, instead of just exchanging people's names, he or she would introduce people by what they do for a living? R.M.*

Are people only "interesting" if they can be of use to you? Has *l'art pour l'art* of friendships gone so completely out the window? For all that, you are right to suggest that it is the responsibility of the host or hostess to make sure guests mix. He or she could provide a conversation opener by following the introduction with an encouraging statement along the lines of, "I'm sure you will have something to discuss since you're both such great opera buffs." I hesitate to urge adopting your recommendation as a hard and fast rule for fear of finding myself at a party one day and overhearing: "Ray, this is Jeremy O'Hara. He's with the police. Jeremy, this is Ray Sloane. He's a dope dealer."

COMMIT ALL THIS TO MEMORY: THERE WILL BE A QUIZ

DEAR EVE: *Everyone has a cross to bear, and mine is that I have a great memory for faces — and a lousy one* *for names. You know that sinking feeling you get at a cocktail mill-in when the time comes to introduce two people you sincerely like, both of whom you were introduced to at the last mill-in six months ago. "Mary Lou, this is ... this is ... uh ..." In the days when honesty was prized above all, I thought it better just to confess my forgetfulness and ask my interlocutor to refresh my memory. My frankness was not appreciated.*

Tell me, is there any gracious way to admit you have forgotten someone's name? Also, you would be doing a merciful deed if you were to coach people whose names have been forgotten on an equally gracious way to supply the necessary information. Send help fast — the next mill-in is rapidly approaching. D.H.

It is problems such as yours which prompted some unsung dolt to unleash a plague of "Hello. My Name Is ..." tags upon the world. I, personally, would prefer to remain utterly anonymous than to have to go around feeling I have been sentenced to summer camp for all eternity. Perhaps some nice things could be said here about those little 24 karat gold ID necklaces which the Debbis of this world all seem to receive on their sixteenth birthdays, but I can't think of any.

I agree that it should be incumbent on the forgettee not to act too uppity toward the forgettor — unless they were previously married to each other. One is only human, for heaven's sake. I watched a woman at a party one night deflect a potentially awkward situation with such grace I could only marvel. The person I was with went up to her and said, "I'm sure I know you from somewhere." The woman supplied her name, and it became quite apparent that my friend had done business with her only a week previous. He was thoroughly mortified at his faux pas, since he was interested in nurturing their professional relationship. "That's quite all right," the woman said. "We met in my office and the circumstances were quite different. I too have difficulty identifying people out of context. I'm sure I wouldn't recognize my family doctor if I were to see him wearing a jogging suit in the park — I'm so used to seeing him in his white coat." Now *that's* good manners.

There are gracious ways to get around one's memory block, but they depend on the circumstances. Your best bet is to seek an ally, someone who does remember or has nothing to lose by asking. For instance, many years ago, I was visiting a friend when her neighbor stopped by. My friend did not introduce us, which I found odd, but when the neighbor returned to her apartment to fetch something, my friend explained she was terribly embarrassed but she couldn't remember the woman's name. This called for guerrilla etiquette. Upon the mystery guest's return, I urged my friend to go off into the kitchen and put the kettle on. I took advantage of her absence by saying, "I'm sorry. Maya forgot to introduce us. I'm Eve and you're ...? When Maya reappeared, I leapt into the breach by announcing, "Maya, *Stephanie* was just telling me that ..." Stephanie and I have been very close ever since, but I have no idea what has become of Maya.

WHO WAS THAT MASKED MAN?

Dear Eve: *The other day I met my girlfriend's landlord for the first time and she said to him, "I'd like you to meet my friend, Sam." That struck me as odd; we're about to share the same apartment — hers — and we're much more than friends. What could she have said? Did she need to describe our relationship to him? S.M.*

I hate to admit that perhaps there is something to "my husband" or "my wife," because I rather like the idea that no one really belongs to anyone else and that we don't all have to get married just to make life simple. But the purpose of introductions is to lay down some ground rules, or establish the parameters, for the relationships which may form as a result. If you are sitting in a restaurant with a female co-worker from the office and your live-in lover happens by, quick thinking is called for. "Julie, what a coincidence. May I present my colleague, Camille Lavoie. We were just discussing the upcoming sales meeting. Camille, this is Julie Duff, the woman I live with."

The woman I live with. The man I live with. It is dreadful, isn't it? There are several cutesy expressions making the rounds which purport to be the answer to this dilemma — co-vivant, paramour, main squeeze — but I can't honestly imagine anyone using them with a straight face. If you like them, feel free.

Unless the introducees really should know each other's relationship to the introducer so that forewarned is forearmed, names alone should be enough. Long-winded whys and wherefores will only serve to confuse.

Your soon-to-be live-in could have made the matter less confusing simply by introducing you with your name only and dropping the gratuitous description of "friend." Her landlord will find out soon enough what the pair of you are up to.

HER NAME IS WOMAN

A little detective work is often part of the name game, especially when it comes to women. Some women are playing by one set of rules and some by another. It used to be easy to tell the score; if she was married she had his name. But today, there's her name, his name and their name, and all three might be different. Throw in a few divorces and remarriages and you get ...

DEAR EVE: *I went to visit a friend recently and discovered his mother was staying with him. She joined us for drinks and was very pleasant company. Unfortunately, when my friend introduced us, he simply said, "This is my mother." No name. I suppose I could have assumed that her name was the same as his, but I was afraid of being wrong, so I just avoided addressing her all night. What should I have done? C.R.*

You were quite right not to have assumed anything. For all you knew, she could have been thrice divorced and remarried since producing your friend (whom, I might add, she doesn't seem to have done a very good job of bringing up). Or, for all I know, your friend might be a member of a Hare Krishna sect who has changed his name, and I can't see a sweet, white-haired, WASPy matron (speaking of assumptions) responding to "Mrs. Anandmurti," unless, of course, she had remarried a Hindu.

It's all so terribly complicated these days; you were wise not to take any chances. Although your friend put you at a considerable disadvantage, there were some tactics you could have tried to ferret out his mother's name. Right after the (non) introduction, you could have stuck your neck out and said, "I'm sorry. I didn't catch your name."

My preferred solution would be to address her as "Ma'am." It smacks a bit of life on the plantation, but it's a marvelous invention that can't fail: she would either have found you delightfully old-fashioned, or she would have said, "You don't have to be so formal. Please call me Rose." And you would have come off smelling like one.

All right, so how *do* you introduce your mother? I've certainly never addressed my mother by her first name, and it would feel strange to refer to her thus, especially to someone my own age. By the same token, I can hardly expect my chum to call her "Mom" just because I do. Even though it might seem excessively formal today, when people are on a first-name basis right off the bat, I still hold with introducing her by her first and last name with a "Mrs." affixed in front. This gives everyone concerned all sorts of options; the person you've introduced her to can jump right in and call her by her first name, or play it cautious and call her Mrs. Whatever until she suggests otherwise. You're off the hook; they now all know who they are. Go mix the drinks.

Women are both troubled and troublesome when it comes to their identities, and one has to proceed gingerly. One evening, while attending one of the myriad chic events that constitute my giddy social life, I couldn't help overhearing the following brief interchange: "Hello, I'm Harold Hardacre." "And I," piped up a small woman on his right, "am the wife of Harold Hardacre."

It's the sort of thing I wouldn't have noticed a few years ago, but (perhaps because there was so little else at this party to hold my attention — this society whirl is hardly what it's cracked up to be) I found myself fretting all night about the insubstantiality of Mr. Hardacre's companion. I wondered if all her towels are monogrammed W of H H. Has she officially changed her name from Susan or Joan or Anne? Does the secretary at the dentist's office pencil in "Wife of Harold Hardacre: 10 a.m." when she calls to make an appointment? Do invitations to parties arrive at their home addressed to Harold Hardacre and Wife? Mostly I wondered what kind of person would so willingly submit to living such a shadowy life.

All of which begs the question: short of giving a lecture on Our Changing Times, what does one do when dealing with the wives of the Harold Hardacres of this world? Or the Mrs. John, Robert, Stanley and George Smiths? One must either assume that it was fashionable for parents to give their daughters masculine Christian names at one point (circa 1927 I'd guess, judging by the preponderance of such monikers among women of "a certain age") or, and it's more likely the case, that such women are not comfortable with any persona other than the one they acquired on their wedding day. So, when introduced to a Mrs. Male Name, it behooves you to address her the way she chooses to be addressed. It may not be good feminism, but it is good manners.

PUTTING IT IN WRITING

Letter writing presents a more difficult problem because there's often nothing to alert you to the recipient's preferred form of address. One letter I received opened with "Dear Madam" and closed with an apology: "As I don't know whether you are Miss or Mrs. (and I abominate Ms), I have done to you what I hate being done to me."

Coincidentally, another letter that arrived on the same day avoided the problem altogether and launched straight into the issue:

> *Could you please tell me the present acceptable way to address a woman in writing? Being born in early 1900, I was taught to address a married woman or a widow as Mrs. William Smith and a divorced woman, Mrs. Mary Smith. Am I out of date? My granddaughter says it is correct to address any woman by her given name rather than her husband's, regardless of her status. Mrs. E.G.G.*
>
> A little giggle follows the signature: *There I go, you see. My husband's name is Eugene George!*
>
> Well, Mrs. E.G.G., your granddaughter is right in principle. But since you so obviously feel more comfortable with your husband's initials than your own, and I'm sure there are thousands like you, I suggest you carry on as you always have, unless someone specifically requests otherwise. No one can fail to see your salutations as anything more than a politesse which may have been superseded by other forms but which is preferable to none at all.

It is certainly preferable to "Dear Madam." Whenever I receive a letter addressed to me thus, I feel it should be carried in to me on a silver platter as I lounge on a crimson velvet sofa wearing a black negligée, a string of pearls and a feather boa, eating chocolates and petting my cat, Frou-Frou.

I have always encouraged informality and the use of just my Christian name in private, and I find this is becoming more acceptable in general. In the business world, things still aren't so easygoing. When writing to a woman of unknown marital status, I find it best to address her by both her first and family name, with no title at all, which in my case would be "Dear Eve Drobot." It is women who are liberated enough to be in business in the first place who most object to being pegged by the existence or non-existence of a Mr. in their lives. You shouldn't deny them the "Dr." in front of their names when they have earned that honorific. If that option exists, it's a great way out.

Dear Eve: *A while ago I met a woman who was introduced to me as Anne Smith-Jones. I need to write a letter to both her and her husband but I have no idea how to address it. Should I assume her husband's name is also hyphenated, or do you think her name is Smith and his is Jones and she combined the two when they got married? Or do you think it's possible that it is her maiden name (which she has kept) and his is something else altogether? M.F.*

Don't assume anything. Also forget the Bard's "a rose by any other name" nonsense. People are *very* particular when it comes to their labels. I go into a snit whenever anyone calls me Evie or supposes my surname has been shortened from something else (it hasn't). Mispronunciations can be countenanced and corrected gently, but when you're committing something to paper, you had better be right.

If the woman is in town, you would earn brownie points for sensitivity by calling her and explaining your dilemma. If that's not practical, skirt the issue by writing only to her for now and asking her to pass a message on to her husband on your behalf. When and if you meet again, do discuss the matter with her. She can only be grateful that you are punctilious enough to want to refer to her husband as he himself wishes to be referred to.

WHAT HAS WOMEN'S LIBERATION WROUGHT?

The issue of who should be called what has become so complicated that newspapers are dealing with it on their editorial pages. One such wizard, in his infinite wisdom, decreed it okay for a woman to keep her maiden name after marriage and for a couple to name their offspring with a hyphenated combination of His and Hers. "We can see the spread of the hyphenated compromise getting out of hand," the editorialist allowed, "as generation by generation, hyphens proliferate in geometric progression; still, the principle of keeping options open on both sides is sound enough."

It's easy for him to say. He won't have to sort out the mess that's bound to result. Can we look forward to grandchildren who have so many hyphens in their names they'll all be known as "Dash" for short? For those who shudder at a vision of the future populated by people who part their names in the middle, I would like to suggest that we look abroad for a perfectly acceptable solution to the inevitable confusion. The Russians (as in so many other things) are of no use to us;

their *ovitches* ("son of") *ovas* ("wife of") and *ovs* ("of the family of") are just too much of a mouthful. I got to page 110 of *Anna Karenina* before I realized that four characters I had so much trouble keeping track *ov* were all the same person.

The Scandinavians have been at the equality game for quite a while now. Their solution at one point was to have the sons named after the father (Olofson) and the daughters named after the mother (Margaretdottor), but that eventually proved too awkward and the practice has been abandoned.

For my money, it's the members of the Spanish aristocracy who have the answer. For centuries now, they have been using a system that lets everyone know who's who without losing track of where everybody came from. When a Garcia marries a Lopez, the progeny are officially called Garcia y Lopez but known only as Garcia. When a Garcia y Lopez marries a Gonzalez y Vega, their issue is named Garcia y Gonzalez, and so on into infinity. Widows need never worry about who they are because they will always have their maiden name to remind them when they bury the *y* part along with their deceased husbands. And they can simply stick a new one on should they remarry. It's a sort of knit one, drop one nomenclature. The system has always worked for them, and there's no reason why it shouldn't work for us.

Our names set us apart, give us our identity, our individuality, our humanity. It is important to learn someone's name and to use it correctly as a way of acknowledging his or her uniqueness. Every relationship, no matter how ultimately unimportant it proves to be, begins with an exchange of this basic information. "'You look a littly shy: let me introduce you to that leg of mutton,' said the Red Queen to Alice. 'Alice — Mutton: Mutton — Alice.' [And when all concerned knew where they stood, Alice asked her hostess if she would like a slice.] 'Certainly not,' the Red Queen said, very decidedly: 'it isn't etiquette to cut anyone you've been introduced to.'"

CHAPTER TWO

The War Between the Sexes

Dispatches from the Front

There's a strong case to be made that men have no manners at all except in deference to the ladies. Politesse and sexual politics have always been inextricably intertwined; exaggerated concern for women's delicate sensibilities has been used for centuries as a way of keeping them out of the smoke-filled rooms where domains were decided, the operating rooms where human lives were mended, the boardrooms where fortunes were made — anywhere, in fact, behind the scenes where men could be found exercising power.

I use the word "ladies" advisedly — it is precisely because women have decided to become full-fledged human beings instead of fragile Dresden figurines that all hell has broken loose on the door-opening front. The saddest argument ever put forward against letting women go about their own lives as they wish is a book called *The Naked Nomads: Unmarried Men in America* by George Gilder. Gilder's thesis, once pared of its high-falutin' sociological trappings, is very basic: because boys will be boys, women must devote themselves full time to keeping men on a tight rein. Otherwise they are apt to misbehave in the most appalling ways.

In the past, women did accept the job of dictating manners. Denied a role in society, they created Society. With minds unfettered by such preoccupations as war, finance and the fate of Bosnia and Hercegovina, they could devote themselves to the real issues of life: proper behavior and who sits next to whom at the dinner table. This was power in its rawest form. If you doubt it, you have only to flip through your college history books. Cardinal Richelieu, back in 1635, was so threatened by the stranglehold the fine ladies of France had on matters moral and cultural that he created the all-male Académie française — just a place where the fellas could hang out and discuss things literary without having to worry about messing up the Marquise de Rambouillet's fancy carpets with their dirty boots and cigar ashes. His treachery finally caught up with him in 1980 when Marguerite Yourcenar was appointed the first female Immortal.

The Académie has changed and so has the rest of life. Women are everywhere these days — in the smoke-filled rooms, in the operating rooms and in the boardrooms. They've had to fight to get there and they intend to stay. The huge issues of who has power and why are still being wrangled over, and as a result, the minute issues, such as who lights whose cigarette, have become fraught with political implications.

I know men who are as strongly feminist in their ideas as Kate Millett, yet who spend an inordinate amount of time wondering if a woman will be offended if they help her on with her coat. I've actually had men say, "I hope you aren't one of those 'libbers'" as they relieved me of a box of books. I don't blame them for their confusion. There are a lot of women who want it both ways; they want the symbolic door to an important job held open for them, but they also expect a male companion to hold the car door open for them on a date.

My attitude is that good manners are not, by definition, something only men extend to women. No one should withhold common courtesy from anyone else as a way of making a political statement. Women should learn not only to open their own doors, but to hold doors open for others, whether male or female. Men should go on being as gracious as they know how and, if they encounter a woman who finds it difficult to accept graciousness gracefully, they should consider her unpleasantness as a failing on her part, not on theirs. With any luck, when the rhetorical dust finally settles, men and women will realize that politeness merely greases the wheels of human interaction, and consideration is a virtue that should remain outside the battleground of the sexes.

The questions in this chapter are all related to the issues feminism has raised. Each one deals with etiquette versus equality, and

I have tried to answer them as though the two were not mutually exclusive.

DEAR EVE: *Why don't men ever light women's cigarettes any more? C.T.*

They will, if you ask nicely. Unless, of course, you ask a non-smoker, in which case not only will you not get a light, you'll also probably get a sermon on your wantonly unhealthy ways.

The tone of lament in your query suggests that what you're missing isn't the flicker of a flame but the flicker of an interest in your every move. While I don't think the mere act of lighting a woman's cigarette is patronizing, some women have come to feel the act implies that they're so scatterbrained and disorganized they can't possibly be expected to cope with such a momentous undertaking as striking a match. A lot of the fawning my-poor-delicate-dear stuff we can do without, thank you very much.

The men you encounter these days have probably had their fingers burned once too often by inflamed declarations of independence. If you are old enough to smoke, you are old enough to carry your own matches.

RAISING CONSCIOUSNESS VS. RAISING A FUSS

DEAR EVE: *The other day a man indicated that I should take a vacant seat on the bus. In these liberated times, he may have been unsure whether to offer it; I certainly was confused about accepting it, especially since he had been standing longer than I had. What should you do in such situations?*

It was very kind of him to offer, and I didn't want to hit him with a heavy feminist diatribe, making him regret his kindness. Yet somehow I felt guilty taking the offered seat. W.L.

It was, as you recognized, an act of kindness and probably nothing more. Save your re-education program for the creep at the office who always calls you "dear" or the nosy neighbor who asks you when you're going to get married so you can stop working for a living. You should consider any act of generosity innocent until proven otherwise. Go on — take the seat and offer a heartfelt thank you.

THE SEXISM STOPS HERE

Not all the boundaries between men and women are easily crossed.

The things we do and say betray a reluctance to accept change. Women still have to stand up for their rights in certain situations. The problem is finding a balance between justified grievance and overreaction. I have attended, to my horror, dinner parties given by people in their early thirties where, as soon as the dishes were cleared off the table, the men retired to another room. I suppose they sat in there drinking brandies and smoking cigars or whatever it is they used to do in nineteenth-century novels. The door had been shut quite firmly in the faces of the "ladies," and they had no choice but to retire to the kitchen.

After-dinner segregation of the sexes is still a fact of life in protocol-minded places such as Washington or Ottawa. Since it is an upper-crusty sort of practice, you could avoid it by limiting your circle of friends to lowlifes as I have done. Terribly proper people never make a fuss. Terribly proper people are also bored to death most of the time. *Somebody* has to refuse to sit at the back of the bus so that this sort of nonsense will come to an end. Any woman who hears at the end of a meal that "the gentlemen will now withdraw to the library" should march right in there with them, pour herself a snifter, plunk herself down in a wing chair and inquire, as she daintily crosses her legs, "Do you have any Havana cigars?"

***DEAR EVE:** While chatting up a woman with fetching eyes at a party, I happened to use the generic "he" in reference to "mankind" (it was that kind of party). Whereupon I was told, stridently, that I was a male chauvinist pig. The question, alas too late, is: should I have set up a pathetic display of whimpering that I'm really a nice guy or should I have happily bashed her in the teeth and be done with it? G.G.F.*

As much as I dislike the phrase (it dishonors both Nicholas Chauvin, the silly little French footsoldier who lent his name to blind loyalty and our porcine friends), you certainly are a male chauvinist pig. Listen to yourself: "chatting up" (instead of "talking to"), "a pathetic display of whimpering" and so on.

The language is fortunately changing to reflect certain basic facts of life, such as the detail that women account for 50 percent of *man*kind. I don't think we need go into contortions to avoid offending — a perfectly decent and acceptable name such as Truman doesn't benefit from being liberated into Truperson — but those who argue things should remain the way they have been because they were always so would probably have disliked doing away with child labor in the 1800s.

I agree that stridency is unpleasant. The woman you were, ahem, chatting up, was wrong to have reacted as fiercely as she did. I can't help but wonder, though, if the discussion had been in any area other than the battlefield of the sexes, whether this would be an issue at all. If she had, say, corrected your misuse of the word "hopefully," would you have written to me?

DEAR EVE: *One of my husband's best friends insists on telling dirty jokes. I'm not a prude, but they're not funny, just sexist. Is there any way I can let him know I don't approve without having him accuse me of being uptight? A.L.*

Don't laugh.

THINGS USED TO BE SO SIMPLE

There seems to be nothing left in our lives which isn't fraught with political implications. For example, I once received a letter which seemed quite straightforward, and was on the verge of answering it in my usual blithe fashion when an alarm bell suddenly went off.

DEAR EVE: *I'm an undergraduate student and I have developed a real crush on one of my lecturers, a doctoral student not much older than I. We talk quite a bit after classes and it's all very friendly, but I'd like to break through to him on a more personal level. Friends tell me to ask him out for coffee, but I just can't think of a cool way to do that. Could you advise me? M.T.B.*

Several years ago, this one would have been a snap. But that was before the whole notion of sexual harassment came along to muddy the waters of relationships. Putting aside, for the moment, the entire discussion of whether Freud was right in suggesting women are constantly looking for Daddy when they insist on falling in love with their doctors, lawyers, teachers or anyone else who is in a position to shake a stick of authority at them, let us consider just how complicated things have become.

Let's reverse the situation. You are a young man trying to forge an academic career for yourself and it's not quite the easy path to a sinecure it once was. A pretty young woman in the third row hangs on your every pronouncement. She's there after each class to probe you further on the impact of the Luddites on subsequent English imperialism. One day, she asks you to have coffee with her and drops all intellectual pretense. The universe unfolds as it should for a while until, for all the usual tawdry reasons, you go your separate ways. She doesn't perform as well as she should on the final exam, and you decide to put your integrity on the line by giving her a low grade.

Hell hath no fury etc., etc., and the next thing you know, you're on the carpet for using your position to obtain sexual favors. She has the campus feminists on her side, and you can kiss your dreams of tenure good-bye.

In other words, if he rejects your overtures, there might be a lot more at issue than your attractiveness. If you take your chances (and I would advise you to because I would hate to see rules and regulations laid down about how people should enjoy each other), you must be prepared to play fair. I realize that all manner of militant feminists are going to be angry with me for saying that, and I don't for a moment mean to imply that there aren't unscrupulous men around who resort to blackmail to satisfy their needs, but I feel that our best defense as women is to stop thinking of our sexuality as a commodity. One should enjoy freely or not enjoy at all. Now I'll get off my soapbox and suggest you simply ask the young man out for coffee as your friends have recommended. There is no cool way to begin a friendship, there are only honest ways. You pays yer money and you takes yer chances.

Whereupon, our far-flung correspondents promptly added their two cents' worth of indignation to the discussion:

DEAR EVE: *I think you made a mistake in the advice you gave the undergraduate student who is interested in her instructor. As you pointed out, grad students and professors are aware of the dangers of sexual harassment. As a graduate student myself, I think the correct advice would have been to suggest the woman approach the lecturer after the course is completed. If the candle cannot burn that long, perhaps it shouldn't have been lit in the first place. Once the course is over and done with, the man will not have any reason to be suspicious of the student's motives. He will not have to wrestle with his conscience when it comes to the final grading or worry about possible repercussions. While you correctly point out these problems, you incorrectly assume that your admonition to the girl to "play fair" will eliminate them.*

I think your position may, in fact, end up doing more harm than good. I hope you will give some consideration to my opinion and reconsider your reply. While you may not feel that a public reversal is in order (how are you at triple salchows?), I at least hope you will take some of the arguments here seriously. B.Y.

I don't even know what a triple salchow is. Oh waiter — another double, please. Your argument is perfectly reasonable, Sir, and I quite agree. Thank you for writing. Class dismissed.

But the student/professor controversy raged on:

DEAR EVE: *The letter written by B.Y. in response to your advice intrigued me. I have been an undergrad, a grad, an instructor and am now somewhat employed by an institution of higher learning so I have some observations to make after years of watching the scene.*

Basically, I agree with B.Y. and see sexual harassment as a problem for women in places of work and education. However, there is another side to the issue which could be summed up as "conflict of interest." Can a professor who is involved with a student possibly be trusted to give her a fair mark, and aren't all the other students at a disadvantage? One might even go further and say that such a female student can have a great advantage when taking a class from any colleague of the professor with whom she is living (or whatever).

I am proud of getting my education honestly and yet I am resentful that such situations exist. I don't know what the solution is. University guidelines on conflict of interest? M.G.O.

There are men who own television stations who give their wives jobs as hostesses of talk shows; there are fathers who buy their daughters hockey teams for their birthdays; there are men who leapfrog to important positions in companies over the heads of people who have worked there for twice as long because Daddy went to school with the boss. All these situations are uncomfortable for people who get where they are by dint of intelligence, diligence, talent and energy. I don't approve, but life's just not fair.

AND LIVE TO TELL THE TALE

DEAR EVE: *Does a woman send a gentleman flowers? If so, under what conditions? J.W.*

Yes. On the occasion of his funeral.

CHAPTER THREE

The Dating Business

The Dating Game is a misnomer. The process of getting to know a member of the opposite sex in order to decide on his or her ultimate suitability for sharing laundry duties should more aptly be called the Dating Business. The process, after all, is ruled by the law of supply and demand ("Are you busy these days?"), entered into by negotiation ("Should I meet you there or would you like me to pick you up?"), operates on the barter system (do two drinks equal a goodnight kiss?) and can potentially lead to a merger or some sort of contract. And there is always a bottom line.

The basic commodities being exchanged have remained the same: sex and security. But the advent of women's liberation has led to a revision in the way deals are made. The rules of the marketplace have changed drastically, and as a result old-fashioned hustlers (of both sexes) have been caught off guard and are having a hell of a time understanding why nobody's buying what they have to sell.

A lot of people I know have all but opted out of The Business. "I don't date anymore" has become such a common refrain that I'm amazed someone like Barry Manilow hasn't already worked it into a hit single (pun fully intended). Others have become cautious. One friend of mine has devised an eminently sensible scheme: she never accepts dinner invitations the first time out. Instead, she suggests that the potential suitor meet her for a late night cup of coffee. He is thus spared the burden of going into hock to impress her with his largesse, while she limits the amount of time she spends with company that might prove to be less than desirable. If, over the strudel, they discover they are both Fellini fanatics, subsequent arrangements can be made. If it proves to be yawn city in spite of all that caffeine, then $3.50 for pastry, a half hour of one's time and a firm handshake aren't all that enormous an investment.

FOR $3, YOU DON'T GET MUCH THESE DAYS

Dear Eve: *Who pays? I hate feeling obligated to a man just because he insists on picking up the cheque but, on the other hand, my financial resources are limited. I just can't afford to spend fifty dollars on a meal because he did last week and I want to even up the score. And I find the process of divvying up the bill while supercilious waiters hover humiliating.*

Also, the rules seem to be different, depending on whom one goes out with. Younger men always assume you're going to pay your own way, while the older ones can't seem to get over their upbringing and insist on paying for everything. Could you suggest a rule of thumb? L.H.

On the whole, men still earn considerably more money than women, and this fact is not to be overlooked when making entries in the dating ledger. I'm not quite advocating from each according to his abilities to each according to her needs, but I think you should be able to cough up only what you honestly can.

If your companion earns double what you do, pay every third time. (Reverse the formula if he's in dire straits but his company is worth it.) Don't forget to take into account the times money doesn't change hands in public, such as when you cook for him or vice versa.

I wish this kind of baroque bookkeeping could be done away with. I'm at a complete loss when it comes to calculating the value of an afternoon walk in the park, or whether three back rubs add up to a weekend at his ski chalet. I say it's spinach, and I say to hell with it. If he wants to pay for eggs florentine, let him. Only you and your conscience can decide what the going price is for your integrity. If it's not on the selling block to begin with, it can't be bought.

Dear Eve: *I have taken a number of young ladies out to dinner on first dates in the past few months, and all of them have extolled the virtues of women's liberation. However, when the tab came, almost none of them offered to pay half or even part of the bill. I earn a good living, but many of these ladies can afford it as well as I can. I'm liberated enough not to expect sexual favors because I've paid. How do I find out if she's liberated enough not to expect to be paid for her company? It would be nice to go out with someone without being stuck with the entire financial responsibility for the evening.*

The first date is usually a time when we're checking each other out. In at least half the cases, either one or the other will not want to waste time seeing that person again. So it's meaningless to suggest that I pay one time and tell the woman the next one's on her. E.F.C.

This sort of misunderstanding is precisely the reason I frown on dinner dates as introductory get-togethers. Have you ever considered the problem as one between guest and host rather than one between men and women? Your dates' confusion might stem from the fact that it is customary for the person who asks to provide, unless stated otherwise at the outset. Think of it this way: if you were invited to someone's home, you wouldn't expect to be asked for a contribution to the grocery bill, now would you? Asking a person to have dinner with you implies that it's to be at your expense.

My recommendation would be to avoid the issue altogether if it bothers you so much. Instead of dinner, the next time ask the object of your affections if she'd like to get together in general and what she'd like to do in particular. Who knows? Perhaps all of these ladies would much rather have gone roller skating.

IS THAT YOUR YELLOW HONDA IN FRONT OF THE FIRE HYDRANT?

Dear Eve: *Parking tickets are ruining my love life. Half the time, when I spend the night at my beau's apartment, I find a loathsome tag on my windshield to spoil the morning. When he spends the night at my place, he gets them too. This habit is running us each about fifty dollars a month on top of the usual dating expenses, and it has touched off an elaborate game about whose place is better suited to our rendezvous. My question is:*

who pays for the tickets? I'm not ready to plunk down the cash to rent him a spot in my building's garage and shock the superintendent. P.K.

The parking ticket as a sign of commitment is a new one to me. Used to be you went to the high school dance, he gave you his ring, you got married. Now it's parking spaces and keys to the garage. What next? "I love you, darling. I want you to have my Mobil credit card"?

I'm also amazed that anyone in this day and age is worried about shocking the superintendent. Believe me, there's nothing he hasn't already seen. If you're serious about this man, by all means rent him the space or, better yet, move in together and become a one-car family. If you're not willing to go to such extremes, I'm afraid you're each responsible for your own parking tickets.

Such annoyances are one of the hazards of urban romance, but they pale before its joys, such as phoning for a late-night pizza *pour deux*. You and your beau might take a tip from the boy who brings it around — pick up and deliver.

A LITTLE ROLE REVERSAL, MY DEAR

Dear Eve: *Now that it is acceptable for women to ask men out, is there an appropriate way of declining an invitation? J.S.*

Well, you can't very well resort to the tried-and-true "Sorry, I'm washing my hair tonight" unless you're a baseball superstar whose windblown coiffure requires a two-hour session with the blow-dryer. Nor will a virile variation on the theme, such as "I have to stay home to shave," really do the trick. Honesty, mistakenly believed to be the best policy, should only be applied in certain cases. If you don't want to go out with a co-worker because you don't believe in mixing business with pleasure, feel free to say so. If, however, you find the lady in question singularly unappealing, a simple "I'm sorry. I'm busy" will suffice. The more you try to explain and justify, the more unlikely she is to take no for an answer and the more likely you are to hurt her feelings.

No one likes to say "no," much less be said "no" to. You can console yourself with the thought that you've had to take your lumps all these years, now it's somebody else's turn. Sauce for the gander and all that. Hollandaise? Béchamel? I never did figure it out.

DEAR EVE: *Is it all right to call a man after a first date if he hasn't called you back? K.H.*

It depends if you picked up your share of the tab. Whoa — down, everybody, down — I'm only kidding.

Of course it's all right, if you're prepared to accept the consequences. You should, however, call with a purpose, not just because your dialing finger is itchy. Call to say thank you or to offer to return the favor. If he's pleased you took the initiative, it will have been a risk worth taking. If he reacts badly, who needs someone whose ego is so mired in the muck of machismo?

SHE'S JUST A GIRL WHO CAN'T SAY YES

DEAR EVE: *Does every date have to end in bed? Even though I make a point of paying my own way so as to eliminate any sense of obligation, I still find it difficult to say no at the end of an evening without the man thinking I never want to see him again. There are just times when I don't feel like sex but that doesn't mean it will always be the case. How can I communicate this without hurting my date's feelings? T.D.*

By saying so. It's not so much what you say as where and how you choose to say it. If you accept his offer of a nightcap at his place after the movie or dinner or three laps around the jogging track, then proceed to down two jiggers of Jack Daniels, take off your shoes and let your hair down, your "no" won't carry much weight.

At the end of the evening, if indeed you do want the evening to end, head for home. If he accompanies you there, say your farewells on the doorstep. A sincere "Thank you, I've enjoyed the evening" might seem like a brush-off, so why not throw in something along the lines of "That was fun. Why don't we do it again soon? Next Thursday is a good night for me, so why don't I give you a call?" If you add a genuinely fond but, for the time being, chaste hug, he'll get the message. Proceed with sureness of purpose across your threshold. When next Thursday rolls around, buy a bottle of perfume.

DEAR EVE: *I am a middle-aged woman who has been widowed for several years. I have only just begun to* *go out with men again, and I have a very basic question: is it okay to kiss on the first date? I don't mean to sound so elementary, but there are two good reasons I ask. The first is that I know dating has changed a lot since the last time a beau came round to my door with a corsage. The second is that such coyness feels very peculiar after all those years of marriage when you knew what to expect — you and your husband went out to dinner, then came home and went to bed. C.C.*

Of course it's okay to kiss on the first date — and anything else, I dare say. But that's not just because dating has changed, which it certainly has. I imagine you are going out with men your own age, whose memories of how it's done are very much like yours. They are probably as nervous about it as you are. But both of you are well beyond the stage of playing tag with virtue.

You are not under any obligation to do anything which goes against your conscience because a man has paid for dinner, so don't kiss him if you don't mean it. Because you can be sure he has experience, and he must be aware that you don't lack it entirely yourself, he's not likely to think of you as a loose woman if you indulge your desire for human warmth. Please pardon me for resorting to a rather overdone slogan of my generation, but if it feels good, do it.

INTERESTED PARTIES

Dating does not occur in a vacuum. Innocent (and sometimes not so innocent) bystanders become involved, whether you want them to or not.

Dear Eve: *I'm dating a man younger than me — he's twenty-four and I'm thirty-four. We've had a few generational clashes (mostly over music), but other than that, the relationship has been proceeding smoothly for several months. We've had a good laugh at our friends' jibes, but now we're facing something more serious: his parents. I'm old enough not to worry what mine think, but for him, it's still important. He took me home to meet them last week, and while everything was done with utmost politeness and nothing was said, I felt very uncomfortable thinking his mother doesn't approve. Should I try to discuss the situation with her? T.P.S.*

If you're capable of mustering the dignity necessary to attend a rock concert, you're capable of knowing when to let sleeping dogs lie. As you say, it's really his problem if his parents think you are debauching their son, and it's up to him to come to terms with it, not you. I would not make Sunday dinner at their house a habit until his parents fully accept their son's untraditional pursuit of happiness.

DEAR EVE: *My girlfriend has an incredibly foul mouth. When we're alone or with people we know very well, it doesn't bother me in the least because I can meet her epithets and raise her a few. But the other night, some friends of mine who had never met her before were in town. We went to a very posh restaurant where Tugboat Annie proceeded to complain about the service in very colorful terms. It seemed she was incapable of completing a sentence without a four-letter word in there somewhere. My friends (and the waiters) were obviously upset. I didn't say anything when we got home but I felt I had a right to. Any suggestions? W.G.*

Jonathan Swift, not remembered as the most sociable of men, once remarked: "Whoever makes the fewest people uncomfortable has the best manners." Your girlfriend doesn't win the prize.

I don't for a moment underestimate the value of letting off steam; when the phone rings, the doorbell goes and the cat throws up on the rug all within twelve-and-a-half seconds of each other, there's nothing quite like an earthy Anglo-Saxon utterance to relieve the pressure.

There are very few people around who don't know what all those words mean; the question is their appropriateness in a given situation. It's a bit like going naked — an intimacy pleasantly shared with a trusted few but awkward in front of strangers.

Before giving your girlfriend the dressing-down she so richly deserves, ask yourself if she was nervous about meeting your friends. If she was afraid they might not like her, she might have simply made damn sure that they didn't by behaving as badly as she knew how. Shocking people is one way of distancing them. Her language wasn't rude — she was. Tell her so.

A GOODNIGHT KISS DOES NOT A CONTRACT MAKE

Possession might very well be nine-tenths of the law, but possessiveness is an absolute zero in personal relationships. When *An Unmarried*

Woman came out several years ago, everyone raved that it was a marvelous breakthrough in portraying the traumas of singlehood from a feminist point of view. Feminist, my eye. Not only does Jill Clayburgh get to keep the apartment with the wrap-around view of Manhattan on a part-time salary, but no sooner does she venture out into the big, bad world of dating than she acquires an avenging knight to restore the honor she had lost to one of them there sexual barracudas — you know, the type that preys on unattached women. When Alan Bates, inexplicably *sans* white horse, and Cliff Gorman, who's so swarthy he's got to be evil, meet at a party, Our Hero beats him up for having dared importune Milady with his advances. That's not feminism — that's feudalism. And it happens all the time. Two drinks and you're mine, baby.

> **DEAR EVE:** *I had been living with a fellow for about a year when we broke up a few months ago. Since then, I've been seeing a man who travels in a completely different social circle. I care for him a great deal, but I don't think we've been together long enough for either of us to assume anything about our relationship.*
>
> *We were recently at a party where I ran into someone I'd met while still with Jeff, my ex. Peter, the man I was with, went off in search of a glass of wine, and I found myself standing alone with my old acquaintance. He didn't seem to have noticed Peter at all and only remarked on Jeff's absence. I informed him we were no longer a pair, which he interpreted as an opening and proceeded to come on to me.*
>
> *Well, okay, so I flirted with him a bit. He's a nice guy and, as I have said, I don't feel that Peter and I are an established couple. But Peter thinks otherwise. He got wind of what was going on, and instead of addressing his complaint to me, dragged my friend off into the backyard and threatened him if he didn't leave me alone.*
>
> *I found all this a bit much. Do you think I should tell him so? D.R.*

A bit much? A *bit* much? Good grief, it's outrageous! Why doesn't he have labels made up to stick all over you which say "Private Property — Keep Out"? Or better yet, why doesn't he put you in *purdah*, that fine Islamic custom of keeping women behind closed doors?

It's time men stopped squabbling over women like dogs over a bone. You, unlike the bone, are an animate object. (I'm sorry, I didn't mean to say you are any sort of an object at all, but that's the way the simile came out.) I think it's a measure of how little some men recognize the existence of a woman's free will that they blame other men for disappointments in a relationship. From where I sit, there's no such thing as stealing someone's woman (or man, for that matter). She goes because she wants to, and knowing someone else is available only makes the going easier.

If Peter finds your tendency to flirt difficult to live with, you're going to have to work it out between yourselves. There's no point dragging a (relatively) innocent third party into the argument. There's only room for two in center ring: anyone else is just a spectator.

THE BOTTOM LINE

ITEM: A man has a pair of tickets to a World Series game in Philadelphia. He asks several of his friends to accompany him, but no one is free. Finally, he decides it would be the perfect opportunity to dazzle a woman he has designs on. He puts a package deal to her: airfare, hotel accommodation, plus great baseball. She questions his motives, but he assures her — No Strings Attached. Off they go into the wild blue yonder and, as far as anyone can tell, have a perfectly wonderful time.

When they return, he regales his friends with tales of their "dirty weekend." He figures the trip made their relationship official and proceeds on the assumption that they are now a couple. When word of this gets back to her, however, she begs to differ. Confrontation, accusation, counter-accusation — an entire display of emotional pyrotechnics. They are (not to put too fine a point on the matter) no longer friends.

A week later, he sends her a bill for her share of the airfare, hotel accommodation and great baseball.

ITEM: They meet and fall madly in love. No ocean too deep, no mountain too high, and all that highly overdone stuff. She's poor and starving; he makes good money. What's mine is yours, etc., etc. She has a rickety old jalopy she loves dearly. It breaks down and she can't afford to have it fixed. "My darling," he says, "let me help you out. Here, take whatever you need." She accepts.

They're no longer madly in love. "You're not the person I thought you were," and all *that* highly overdone stuff. Six months after the teary good-byes, she runs into a mutual friend. "Saw your ex the other day," says the friend. "Oh, and how is he? she asks. "He's fine.

Except he's telling everybody who knows you that he lent you a hundred dollars to get your car fixed and you never paid him back."

ITEM: A man and a woman live together. Her holidays are coming up and she has her heart set on a trip to the Caribbean — with him. "Just the two of us, lazing on the beach drinking piña coladas." But his money is all tied up. "No problem," says she. "It'll be my treat." He offers to pay her back when his term deposits mature or his ship comes in or whatever. She pooh-poohs the idea, insisting his company is worth it to her.

Some time after the vacation, they decide not to live together any longer. As he's sorting through the bookshelves trying to figure out if a certain copy of *In Patagonia* is his or the one her brother gave her for Christmas, she appears in the doorway. "When do you think you'll be able to reimburse me for the trip?" she asks.

I have no mind for high finance, especially when it comes to relationships. I find it astounding that what might be a simple financial arrangement when conducted between friends becomes something else altogether between lovers. Bad debts are bad manners enough, but turning a gift into a debt is worse still. When we were kids, we used to call it Indian giving.

It's a bizarre bit of adding and subtracting that turns a love object into a liability. The formula goes something like this: I invested in you, you didn't live up to my expectations, I want my money back. Yet, I don't think anyone has ever entered into a relationship with the understanding that they'll get a refund if things don't work out. And just how satisfying can an affair be if one of the lovers has a meter running? It quickly goes from billing and cooing to just billing. (Good-bye, darling. Thanks for the memories. I'll have my accountant call you in the morning.)

I'm not so sure it's dollars and cents ex-lovers are after. They want some sort of satisfaction for bruised feelings and shattered plans. But they'll settle for hard currency. Unfortunately, it doesn't work that way. Money is a cheap way of getting revenge.

If you find yourself on the receiving end of a bill, instead of a *billet doux*, you are within your rights to ignore it. Should your ex persist, say you'd be perfectly willing to discuss it — in small claims court.

CHAPTER FOUR

Bedside Manners

Parental guidance is recommended for this chapter. If you don't have children to advise, or you can't borrow any for the occasion, at least pull the blinds down.

I usually avoid sex. Writing about it, that is. But the queries I have received on the subject have led me to the inescapable conclusion that bedside manners are the only ones that really count. A friend has observed that no matter how refined a man might seem at the dinner table, if he undresses without taking his watch and socks off first, he just ain't got no couth. And my father is fond of saying that a true gentleman is revealed by his behavior in the jungle, not in the drawing room. From what I've seen and heard of bedrooms in recent times, I'd say it's a jungle in there.

FOR OPENERS

Call it candor, openness or "being upfront" — enough's enough. People are saying the most astounding things to one another these days, and I don't think it has added one whit to the quality of human relationships.

Dear Eve: *I like to think that I've kept pace with the sexual revolution; that, if I'm not exactly up for anything, at least nothing surprises me. That was true until last week. At a friend's house I met* X, *handsome, witty, cultivated, charming and very sexy. We had a good flirt. He spoke, in passing, of his marriage as a comfortable, open arrangement. Since I'm not looking for a husband and had in mind nothing that would threaten a man's domestic felicity, I cheerfully accepted his invitation to lunch. Lunch was titillating and fun. I found myself looking forward to the drama unfolding. Three days later, he telephoned and said, without preamble, "I've been thinking about you. Will you go to bed with me?" Tell me, am I being old-fashioned in finding this approach somewhat lacking in class? G.A.*

I've heard of telephone solicitations before, but I always thought they had something to do with magazine subscriptions. Pardon my naïveté. They say the shortest distance between two points is a straight line, and that's the straightest line I've ever heard. It obviously didn't succeed in bringing the two of you closer, so the fellow not only needs to brush up on his manners but on his trigonometry as well.

Since adultery per se is somewhat lacking in class, if one is going to indulge in it at all, one ought to compensate by doing it with as much elegance and finesse as possible. The most common rationalization for doing it in the first place is: "The romance has gone out of my marriage." So I'm at a total loss to understand why someone would go out of his way to take the romance out of a fling before it had even begun. I'm as old-fashioned as you in believing that a bit of beating around the bush can create the excitement necessary to make sex seem a little less like brushing one's teeth. His approach carries the recently canonized principle of honesty a bit too far. What's the fun of a tryst without trying?

THE THOUGHT THAT COUNTS

Dear Eve: *It's hard enough to find the appropriate moment and even harder to find the appropriate words to ask a woman whether she is ... uh ... taking precautions. I mean if I have brought some along and suggest we use them, she's going to think I'm an operator, right? Do I assume, the first time around, that she knows what she's doing? How the dickens does one ask? J.P.L.*

She probably knows what she's doing or you wouldn't be in this position. But as far as contraception is concerned, don't assume anything. The mere fact that you are concerned about the subject is to your credit; it means you don't subscribe to what Germaine Greer has dubbed "the spittoon theory of womanhood." First-time lovers often get rave reviews from women I know for asking the question at all, no matter how clumsily.

There is really no appropriate moment since the choreography of each love affair is apt to differ. I would think that as she takes you by the hand to lead you to the bedroom is probably closer to the mark than as you step out the front door on your way to dinner. Intimate subjects should be discussed only at intimate moments.

As for bringing your own supplies, I don't find anything wrong with that as long as you don't arrive brandishing them. (On a first date, do leave your alarm clock and toothbrush at home.) If you are the sort of gracious guest who wouldn't dream of showing up for a dinner party without a bottle of wine, act as though these particular contributions are being offered in the same spirit of consideration. Most women have given the matter a great deal of thought and, if they are not on The Pill, probably have an alternative method at hand. That doesn't mean that they don't enjoy being relieved of the responsibility from time to time.

THE ANSWER TO DR. FREUD'S QUESTION

Once in a while, I receive a letter that is too hot to handle. Manners and sex therapy are not to be confused, and most queries concerning who gets to do what to whom and how are outside the realm of my competence. But one in particular did strike a nerve, so to speak.

DEAR EVE: *Now that the female orgasm is out in the open, it's getting to be a drag to find oneself in bed with a man who stops whatever he is doing every five minutes to ask: "Didja come yet?" Would you please advise your male readers that this form of concern is really quite unnecessary? S.T.J.*

I don't think it is concern. I think it's a slyer and more socially acceptable way of asking "Aren't I terrific?" A man who is genuinely concerned with your satisfaction would allow you to arrive at it in your own good time instead of haranguing you continuously to give him a confirmation of his masculinity. Unfortunately, the kind of men who carve notches in the headboard are still around, although the more sophisticated ones don't just count the women they have bedded, they tally the trips to Nirvana on which they have served as tour guides. The proper response to such a question is: "No, and I probably won't if you don't stop indicating points of interest along the way." Be prepared to seek out a less badgering bedmate.

GOOD CLEAN FUN

DEAR EVE: *What is the protocol of bathing with a friend? Who gets in first? J.P.M.*

The person whose bath it is runs the water and tests it. He or she gets to sit on the tap side. The rubber duck is up for grabs. There should be plenty of fresh towels handy, not to mention a mop.

WHAT GROWN-UPS DO

DEAR EVE: *I am a single mother with two children, aged eight and eleven. Dating is hard enough when you're in my position: I have to pay babysitters and, more importantly, find men to date who aren't scared off by a ready-made family. On top of it all, I find myself worrying about whether I can bring a man home. I rarely do it but I was wondering: should I introduce him to my children when I do? S.G.*

Your children are old enough to know what's going on. I don't subscribe to the martyr theory of motherhood when it comes to one's sexual needs, as long as you haven't gone so far as to install a revolving door in your bedroom. Children are possessed of eyes and ears, not to mention imaginations of extreme sensitivity. Your wisest course is to have them on your side. If you are seeing a man often enough to want to share more than a bucket of popcorn with him at the movies, let your kids in on the pleasure of his company.

One woman I know of, trying to be ultra-discreet, spirited her companion in after she knew her kids were asleep and prevailed upon him to leave before they woke up. The next morning, she went downstairs only to find her ten-year-old fighting back tears at the kitchen table. "What's the matter, honey?" she asked solicitously. "I guess your friend didn't like us," her daughter replied. "He didn't want to stay and have breakfast with us."

WHAT DO YOU LIKE FOR BREAKFAST?

DEAR EVE: *Are there any rules for spending the night at a woman's house for the first time? This happened to me recently, and I didn't know what was expected of me in the morning. Matters were complicated by the fact that she had a roommate who made me feel unwelcome in the kitchen. Any tips for morning-after behavior? P.H.*

I've always felt "Your place or mine?" is a loaded question. At your place, you have the advantage of familiar surroundings, you stand a good chance of finding clean underwear when it's called for and you know fairly accurately what is still edible in the refrigerator. In alien territory, you're only a guest, with more privileges albeit than most, but still a guest. The cardinal rule, if you want to be invited back, is to keep just that in mind. Don't make yourself too much at home. Pull your dirty underwear back on, not to mention your jeans, before venturing out to explore the terrain. Even if she lives alone, in the heat of passion she probably neglected to mention her cleaning woman arrives at 8 a.m.

The bathroom will probably be your first foray. Don't decide to take a long, leisurely bath without consulting the other occupant(s), even if that is your normal matinal practice. The tools of the trade may be temptingly arrayed, but you should still ask permission before you avail yourself of them. People are illogical about their possessions; you might reason that the two of you have already shared all sorts of intimacy, so she can't possibly object to your using her back scrubber, but she might have other ideas. Or you might discover by its unpleasant taste that she uses the toothbrush on the sink to polish her jewelry while the one for oral hygiene is kept in the medicine chest. Get the lay of the land first. And one other very important detail for men who find themselves in an all-female household: don't leave the toilet seat up.

In the kitchen, with someone who was not party to the good times, you're damned if you do and you're damned if you don't. If you help yourself too freely, the roommate might resent your presumption. If you sit around waiting to be served, she is almost certain to resent your imperiousness. Your best bet is to introduce yourself (if your hostess is not present to attend to that duty) and say, "Maggie told me I should help myself to coffee and grapefruit." Permission from HQ will soften the blow of your invasion. Offering to serve *her* coffee might also effect a truce.

Finally, don't disappear on the sly. If you know an early appointment will have you out on the streets before your partner starts to stir, tell her about it before going to sleep. Women hate being snuck out on — it makes them feel cheap.

DEAR EVE: *Please don't get the wrong idea but I have, on occasion, brought a man home from a party because something had started which couldn't be finished in public. But I find that sex is one thing, sleeping is something else again. I just can't get a good night's sleep sharing a bed with someone I don't know very well.*

Is there any tactful way to get him to go home after the purpose for which he was your guest has been ... um ... satisfied? D.V.

I'm amazed that you would think me capable of getting the wrong idea. It is my job to have nothing but the right ones.

There is a tactful way, yes. An easy one, no. You can't expect to kick people out of bed and still have them think you are a fine human being. If you don't care to have him back for an encore performance, you have nothing to lose by being blunt about your need for solo shut-eye. But if you're nurturing notions of an on-going number, you had best proceed with tact.

Tactfulness requires a degree of effort and a degree of deception. If going to sleep with a clear conscience and waking up alone mean that much to you, you are a prime candidate for the Thirty-Third Street Shuffle, a ploy devised by a dear friend at that address who has had many opportunities to develop a foolproof system for such moments of need.

The TTSS is based on the premise that after satisfying one appetite, most healthy people are bound to develop another. Of course, at that hour, there can't be anything in the refrigerator of interest. She just happens to know a twenty-four hour snack bar, a mere crosstown bus ride away, where they have the most divine maple walnut ice cream. She's *gotta* have maple walnut ice cream or she'll *die*!

That gets them dressed, out of the house and — after they've had their ice cream — shifting their feet on the sidewalk. They both have to go to work the next day, so there's no point going back to her place and going through the good-bye routine again in another three or four hours. So they might as well get it over with there and then. "Thanks for the lovely evening. Stay in touch." Phew. Alone at last.

I grant you it's a bit overwrought, but I warned you that it wasn't going to be easy.

FAMILIARITY BREEDS

Dear Eve: *We always eat at my place, no matter where we wind up spending the night. Who should pay for food? Booze? S.O.*

At some point, inevitably, romance wears off and housekeeping takes over. As long as someone is invited to your house, he is a guest and should be treated as such. But when the relationship has gone on long enough to warrant predictability, you're no longer visitors, you're a two-apartment family. That means budgeting and sharing costs. I don't think one person should always wind up performing one specific task, but if that's the way you've arranged things, it must work for you. You might find that the most diplomatic way to bring up the idea of chipping in is to suggest that you buy groceries together and make a weekly jaunt to the supermarket part of your schedule of events. But in the case of personal predilections, the person predilecting should supply. I used to spend time with a man who only drank coffee in the morning and had obviously never met anyone who didn't do likewise. But my preferred brew is tea, so after we had been together a couple of months, I thought nothing of buying a tin of Irish Breakfast and storing it in his kitchen cabinet.

Booze is a touchy subject because it tends to be expensive. If your friend insists on a dry martini before dinner, and you don't indulge, he might notice the conspicuous lack of gin and vermouth. If he comments on this, there's your opening to say, "Oh, I only drink wine or beer. Please feel free to bring over whatever you need." Provide him with an olive to put in his glass.

Dear Eve: *My boyfriend and I maintain separate apartments. Since he leaves for work an hour before I do, I was wondering, when I spend the night at his place, should I make the bed? E.D.*

By all means. Behave as you would if you were a house guest at Aunt Gertrude's. Neatness is always appreciated but resist the temptation to pick up his socks or wash a week's worth of dirty dishes. You wish to be seen as a considerate companion — you are not auditioning for the role of his mother.

CHAPTER FIVE

Party, Party, Party

That's All You Ever Think About, You Hedonist Bunch

Get your Lurex sweater back from the cleaners, fish Grandma's rhinestones out of the jewelry box, glue the heel back on your pink satin pump and polish up your repertoire of repartee — it's party time. Good news for those of you who love to socialize, bad news for those of us who get a hangover by merely looking at a punch bowl.

There are as many kinds of parties as there are people. But whether you find yourself at a housewarming, a celebratory supper ("We're engaged!" "I've been promoted!" "It's the end of term!") or a bash for pages 251 to 1689 inclusive of the telephone book, there is one rule which applies to all festivities: never go empty-handed.

GIVE AS GOOD AS YOU GET

DEAR EVE: *Since people are expected to buy gifts for a host and hostess, could you suggest something safe and inexpensive to bring to someone's house if you don't know them too well? M.R.*

Let's see ... there's wine, and then there's wine, and of course, there's wine. You can bring it in the bottle, you can bring it in a stone crock, you can pour it over peaches and bring it in a Mason jar. You can wrap it up in silver paper; you can tie it with a bow; you can stick it in a basket with bread and brie and homemade mayo. (Ye gods. A poem. The party spirit will make you mad. *Mad* I tell you.)

Wine will certainly do for the first time. But gift-giving is a bit like narcotics; once you start, who knows where it might lead? Consider this cautionary tale.

Two people I know, a husband and wife, went to Jamaica for a holiday. There they met another couple who, it turned out, made their home only a few blocks away from them. The four became fast friends and decided to keep up the relationship once back on home ground. Soon they found themselves having dinner at each other's houses every two weeks or so. And, before they knew it, an elaborate (and ultimately expensive) ritual had been established.

Being well brought up, my friends responded to the first invitation by arriving for dinner bearing a box of chocolates and a bottle of fine wine. A fortnight later, they returned the invitation and found their new friends on the doorstep at the appointed hour with a bouquet of flowers and a case of imported beer. And so, for several months, the four of them worked their way through pounds of pâté, bottles of Sambucca, slivovitz and Sauterne, and Sara Lee's best cherry cheese cake. It got, not to overstate the matter, silly.

Good manners do not require adhering to unnecessary ritual; they require common sense. When it got to the point that my friends were considering pawning their earthly possessions for the sake of a dinner party, they brazenly arrived one night with nothing at all. "Look," said the husband, matter-of-factly, "We're here because we enjoy your company. We are no longer listed on the commodities exchange." Great sighs of relief all around.

DEAR EVE: *How do you firmly yet classily request food and drink offerings for a large party without looking cheap? F.D.*

Obviously, you find that marking the invitation BYOB is not enough. (Have literacy skills declined to that extent? Oh my.) You might try cleverly disguising your intentions by having a theme for your party: instead of specifically requesting vittles and vino, inform your guests that they are required to bring something red to gain admission. The unimaginative types will fall back on a trusty bottle of Burgundy, but the flashier ones might resort to Campari, chili or carnations. All will contribute nicely to the atmosphere.

THOSE THREE LITTLE WORDS

DEAR EVE: *I was invited to a housewarming party recently and arrived (appropriately, I thought) with a set of towels as a gift. When I gave it to the hostess, she became really flustered. She pointed to a stack of packages on a table and said, "I didn't want people to bring presents. I don't know what I'm going to do with all this stuff!" I was very embarrassed and didn't know what to say. Was I wrong to have brought a gift? E.P.*

Coals to Newcastle, pearls before swine — pick the cliché that suits you best. I wouldn't go to another of this woman's parties, much less bring her another gift. You were perfectly correct — housewarmings, baby showers, engagement parties and the like are all gift-giving occasions. In fact, cynics might argue that the only reason for having them is to stock up. Anyone organizing one of these little fêtes should be aware of what to expect. Your hostess could have spared herself the embarrassment of riches by simply marking the invitation "No gifts, please."

GUEST APPEARANCES

DEAR EVE: *I was invited to a brunch one Sunday morning and gladly went in my Sunday best. I should explain that I take the injunction to treat the seventh day of the week as a day of rest rather seriously, so my Sunday best consists of a clean pair of jeans and a T-shirt.*

Most brunches I have been to are laid-back affairs, usually no more than scrambled eggs and a pitcher of Bloody Marys. But I arrived to find everyone else dressed to the nines, and a butler doling out expensive catered food as well as refilling glasses of champagne. I know I shouldn't be complaining, but I felt very out of place in my get-up and was quite uncomfortable because I had not known what to expect. Could you please tell me when it is appropriate to ask a host or hostess what one should wear to a party? A.G.

It is never appropriate. The host or hostess should tell *you*. Your friends did you a disservice by not issuing instructions along with the invitation, and if you spoiled the decor with your dowdy duds, they have no one to blame but themselves.

DEAR EVE: *I once invited a guy to accompany me to a party, and he assumed I meant that he should show up with his entourage. How do you handle the person with the herd instinct? J.W.*

Put him out to pasture. I don't know if it yet qualifies as a trend (I have yet to read an in-depth analysis of it in the *SoHo Weekly News*) but I have noticed that, in response to women's new social aggressiveness, men have taken to arming themselves with bodyguards.

I once met a pleasant fellow who was passing through town and suggested we spend some time together. He arrived at the rendezvous with Athos, Porthos and Aramis (the swashbuckling kind, not the stuff in the bottle). I tried again the next night; Aramis had been cashiered but A & P hung on. On night number three, only one musketeer was left, so I figured — as hopeless as I am with math — that I would surely get d'Artagnan to myself if I could only hold out one more day. He left town the following morning but two weeks later I got a postcard — from Aramis.

Once the whole gang shows up, you have no choice but to be civil. If the party is a come-one, come-all affair, the host or hostess might welcome unfamiliar faces, and the best you can hope for is that the crew will mingle well enough to leave you alone with your date. Or you might meet someone more considerate at the party.

If you know your host or hostess will be annoyed by the multitude, explain the situation to the ringleader and suggest the bunch of you go out for pizza instead. In either case, you should find a moment to inform your friend that party invitations are not the same thing as chain letters.

DEAR EVE: *I was looking forward to a party given by a friend because it was going to be a chance to see and talk to a lot of people I hadn't seen in a long time. But instead of a convivial gathering of old friends, the host turned the volume of his stereo system up to full blast and kept insisting everybody dance. Nobody was up for it and we tried to ignore him, but he gave us a lecture about all the trouble he had gone to rolling up the rug, rearranging the furniture and taping the music. What I'm* *wondering is this: can people who give parties make rules and are guests obliged to follow them? R.O.*

It's his party and he can be a beast if he wants to. Sure a host can make rules — he can decree what time one should arrive, when one should think of leaving, how much alcohol one may consume and whether or what one may smoke on his premises. He may tell you he prefers that you not bring additional guests, that you leave your snow-covered boots out in the corridor or that certain rooms are off limits. But he may not tell you how to enjoy yourself.

Good company, music, food, drinks and sometimes even illicit smoking materials are pleasant perks of party-going. But people have different notions of what constitutes a good time, and the host's duty is to make it possible, not issue a *ukase* on how it is to be done. Your friend gets my nomination for the host with the least.

WRETCHED EXCESS

Dear Eve: *I know the whole idea of a party is to be able to let go and have fun, but for some people that invariably means getting rolling drunk. My parties have never got to the point where the neighbors called the police, but at the last one, two guests thought it would be a riot to relieve themselves on the pavement (and proceeded to do so), one woman spent half an hour in the bathroom (I don't know what she was doing in there, but her dress looked the worse for the experience) and one guy passed out on the living room floor (he was gone before we got up in the morning). I think people are adults and should be responsible for their own behavior, but my wife says we're obliged to look after them. Who's right? G.D.*

Sounds like a fun crowd of people. Your wife's right. Unfortunately, part of the function of a host and hostess is to act as glorified babysitters. Limiting your guests' alcoholic consumption is a thankless task, and I don't recommend it as a solution; you have no way of knowing what anyone's capacity is and you might appear (horror of horrors!) cheap if the booze isn't free-flowing. What you must do is circulate and keep an eye out for signs of sybaritic excess. If you spot someone who is unsteady on his feet, it's time for him to go home — but for heaven's sake, don't let him drive. Try to find another guest who lives in the same direction and say,

"I think Richard could stand to sleep it off. Would you mind giving him a ride home?" If he does mind, call a cab yourself and pay for it.

As for your friend in the living room, he had by his actions (or rather, lack of them) declared himself an overnight guest and should have been treated as such. You should have picked him up off the floor and made him as comfortable as possible on the chesterfield. Even tucked him in with a blanket. When he woke up several hours later, he wouldn't have felt obliged to flee into the night. If you made coffee for him in the morning and lent him your toothbrush, he'd either think you're the greatest friend in the world or be so embarrassed that he would never darken your doorstep again.

TIME, GENTLEMEN, PLEASE

It does happen occasionally, you know — even I manage to commit a faux pas. I dashed home from work one Friday night, doused myself in perfume, pulled on my party frock and set off to boogie. As we approached the house where the bash was to be, the abundance of parking spaces on the street, the bright lights visible through the living room windows and the deadly silence of the summer night signalled that something was very wrong. It was. The party was scheduled for Saturday night.

It reminded me of a story my mother likes to tell of a terribly proper upper-class British couple who decided to throw a costume ball. The evening before the festivities, as they were sitting down to supper, the doorbell rang and shortly thereafter the butler announced the presence of a gentleman in full pirate regalia. They invited him in, asked the butler to set another place at table, and made elegant small talk throughout the cold roast beef and cucumber salad. After a cordial snifter of brandy, they showed him to the door and bade him farewell by saying: "Thank you ever so much for coming. Now be sure not to forget about our fancy dress party tomorrow night. We will be delighted to see you again."

DEAR EVE: *I belong to a single parents' club, and recently the club accepted my offer to use my home for one of their parties. Refreshments were served around midnight, and people started to leave soon after. I had had no particular partner but had been busy as a hostess and had enjoyed myself.*

Then I discovered that the only guests still there were three couples dancing very amorously in the recreation room in very subdued lighting. I literally didn't know where to go or what to do with myself. I sat in the recreation room for a while, but no one paid any attention to me. None of the couples broke up so that I could dance with one of the men, and I began to feel extremely foolish. I went up to the kitchen, but it seemed rather gauche to start doing dishes while my guests danced downstairs. I certainly couldn't go home — I was home! I couldn't go to bed; that would seem equally out of place. I went back downstairs but felt too uncomfortable. In desperation, I returned to the kitchen and read a book. I'm at a loss to know how I should have handled the situation. B.P.S.

Whose house did you say this was? Single parents' club or no single parents' club, the members should have realized they were in somebody else's home and not in a church basement. All the regular rules of party-going and party-giving still apply, and the hostess calls the tune.

Speaking of which, who was minding the music? You could have slipped "The Party's Over" on the turntable as a not-overly-subtle hint that the time had come to dally elsewhere (I assume that we're not dealing here with teenagers and that these people all had homes of their own to go to). Or, if you were simply miffed at being left out of the proceedings, anything by Lesley Gore would have gotten the message across. No record collection is complete without these songs — they didn't get to be hits for nothing, you know.

The best course of action, however, is the most obvious one: turn off the music, turn up the lights, start emptying the ashtrays and picking up the glasses. This will give your guests two choices: they can either give you a hand or leave. Most people leave. In which case, you are free to tidy up and to go to bed with your book.

DEAR EVE: *I hate to go to parties, but sometimes I find I can't tactfully avoid them. My question is this: how soon can I leave? V.W.*

There are two kinds of parties one can't tactfully avoid: gatherings of the clan around oversized poultry and business-related ventures where attendance is taken. If your absence raises eyebrows, a mere two-second appearance will provoke a genuine scandal. If you absolutely must go, you absolutely must go for the duration.

At the large business affairs where you may be lost in a crowd, stay for as long as it takes to make your presence known to anyone likely to be carrying a mental time sheet: your boss, the guest of honor and the office gossip. The time necessary to go through a tall drink ought to do it. Once you've touched base with those who count, there's no need to make excuses for a hasty departure. After a minimum of twenty minutes of hale-fellow-well-met, you can slip away with a clear conscience.

At a sit-down family dinner where everyone must be accounted for, it's not that easy. Unless you warn your host and hostess when the invitation is issued that you'd love to attend, but you may have to vamoose early to catch a train/write a report for an 8 a.m. meeting/tend to your sick mother, you'll have to sit still until at least one glass of cordial has been consumed in the living room after the party has left the table. Small children are a boon in this case; there's always the babysitter to consider. Figure on about two hours' worth of small talk in all before you're home free.

WE OWE IT ALL TO FRIENDSHIP

Dear Eve: *What can be done about those delightful guests you really love to have because they're witty, fun, bright, etc., but who never reciprocate, whether having us over for coffee, out for a drink or even for brunch? We love thowing parties and do so about four times a year but are getting discouraged by the feeling that we are the only ones playing host. J.G.*

Ah yes, that inevitable moment when one tallies the debits and credits in the social ledger. It's *so* depressing. We owe Susan and George one for the weekend at their cottage this summer. Pat and Andrew owe us one for helping them move. It's our turn to have Aunt Edith for Christmas dinner.

To hell with being an accountant, I say. If you like to play host, and your bank account permits it, consider the example of Lady Ottoline Morrell, a turn-of-the-century Englishwoman who didn't have a lot going for her other than a couple of lovely country houses and a guest list interesting enough to secure her a place in history. The names on the list included those of Bertrand Russell, one of her lovers (she complained in a letter to a friend that he had bad breath) as well as those of Augustus John, D.H. Lawrence, Prime Minister Asquith, Aldous Huxley and Lytton Strachey, not all of whom graced her bed as well as her table. There was a time, you see, not so very long ago, when being witty and fun and bright were considered enough to pay the freight.

There are, of course, those social occasions which you must see to and those you enjoy. From now on, divide your dos into two categories: the fun party and the duty party. Invite your indolent friends to the former and spare them the boredom of the latter. Be glad you are able to appreciate their delightful presence and to receive their undying gratitude, if not an invitation by return mail.

CHAPTER SIX

Dinner's at Eight

General party-going rules apply when you find yourself one of the select few seated at a mahogany table bristling with fish forks, floral arrangements and fine china. But the going is tougher, because there are more rules to follow and therefore more ways to go wrong, publicly. Paranoia is usually served before the soup; the minute you sit down, you are struck by the awful awareness that people are watching at close quarters. If you pick up the wrong piece of cutlery, it will be the talk of the town and you know it. Why, oh why, didn't you pay closer attention to your mother when there was still time?

Nonsense. The formality of today's dinners isn't a patch on the strictness of society suppers our parents or, more likely, our grandparents had to put up with if they belonged to the miniscule segment of the population who could afford real silverware. No lounging about in caftans for them — it was all corsets and Eton collars, and stiffness was part and parcel of the ordeal. We have it remarkably easy by comparison.

Dinner parties are simply the most civilized way of getting to know people. Good food, attractive table settings, spirited conversation fueled by ... well, spirits ... all combine to make life worth living for three or four glorious hours. You should go to dinner parties to relax, not to pass an etiquette exam.

But because dinners are intimate, they call for a bit more conscious consideration. If the person on your right offends you, you can't merely wander off in search of more congenial company across the room. But most of all, you must realize that your host and hostess exerted considerably more effort to make the evening a success than putting out bowls of potato chips and taping every Rolling Stones album in their possession.

Being on your best behavior is not that difficult; it is merely a matter of bearing in mind that, for a limited period of time, you are going to be cheek by jowl with others. My theory of table manners is that they were invented specifically for the purpose of leaving the least mess on the table for the overworked servants to pick up. If you stick with me, you'll learn more about knives and forks than you've ever wanted to know. But first, let's consider the dinner party in general and some of its special requirements.

BY INVITATION ONLY

Dear Eve: *Is one obliged to answer an* RSVP *on an invitation, or is it okay just to show up? B.O'R.*

RSVPs and other letters of the alphabet are rarely strewn about for no good reason. Your host may be planning to serve individual coquilles St. Jacques and needs to know how many to make. Or he may want to know whether to set his table in the dining room (where he can seat twelve comfortably) or bring out the card tables in the living room (where he can accommodate sixteen). Save him the headaches. Honoring the RSVP means he won't have to resort to ESP.

Dear Eve: *Short of asking guests over two hours in advance, how do you get them to time their arrival so that the pot roast doesn't get potted? M.P.*

I really don't understand what's so fashionable about arriving late, but I've never known anyone to show up at the appointed hour. I suppose the idea is to convey to the assembled company that one is so astoundingly busy that it is difficult to cram all the living there is to do into such a limited amount of time. But I have known people who will kill a couple of hours at a movie rather than turn up before all their friends have had a good anxious half-hour wondering if they've been in a car accident. Arriving late is only marginally better than arriving too early and catching one's hostess still in her skivvies. At least in the latter circumstances one can offer to set the table or make oneself useful in other ways.

The trick, obviously, is to invite guests for six o'clock, expect them at seven and time dinner for eight.

It is quite correct (though a bit Draconian) to sit down at table when most of those invited have been accounted for and to let the supposedly stylish stragglers feel sheepish about missing the soup. A cook shouldn't be forced to go to the lengths the famed chef Escoffier did when his company insisted on speechifying instead of dining. He prepared soufflé after soufflé at three-minute intervals, intending to have a perfect one on hand when people were finally ready to eat. Ten went into the garbage before *les messieurs* were *servis*. Eggs are just too expensive.

LIPS THAT TOUCH LIQUOR

DEAR EVE: *I always make a point of bringing a bottle of wine when invited to dinner, but we have been asked to the home of some new friends whom I know are absolute teetotallers. I would still like to observe the custom of contributing something to the cause, but I don't want to offend them. Can you suggest some alternatives? K.H.*

All right, I'll admit it. I've sold my soul to the local wine merchant. Try flowers instead. I don't know anyone who doesn't like them (except perhaps Hamlet and hay fever sufferers). A pot of mums or a big bunch of glads will look just as nice on a table as a bottle of Pommard '71 and cost a good deal less.

DEAR EVE: *So many people these days are vegetarians or on salt-free diets or something. When planning a dinner party, is it good manners to ask your guests if they have any dietary requirements? F.M.*

Not only is it good manners, it is practically *de rigueur*.

I once had the misfortune to assume a new-found French friend would be delighted with a meal cooked in the manner of his native land. No sooner did he sit down than he pronounced the anchovies in the salade Niçoise indigestible, informed me he couldn't eat boeuf bourguignon because of his religious principles, his liver would not permit him to sample the wine, the taste of vinegar made him ill, and he was allergic to cheese, especially Camembert. I no longer cook any meals unless I am reasonably certain they are going to be eaten. The wretch was not invited back.

There are a great many reasons why a guest might not eat everything that's put on a plate in front of him, even if you are a terrific cook and wouldn't dream of adding baking soda to the green beans. He may turn down the langoustine because he is allergic to shellfish, a common enough condition, unlike the availability of langoustine. He might pass up dessert because he had a traumatic experience with blanc-mange as a child, or he may cold shoulder your cold shoulder of pork because he is a devout Moslem. But the point is, you can't possibly be expected to cater to these quirks unless you have been warned.

I wish a hostess didn't need to ask. A sensitive guest should volunteer the information about his or her special requirements at the time the invitation is issued. You might realize that it wouldn't be kosher to ask your Jewish friends to a backyard barbecue where the starring attraction is a mess of ribs, but you're not expected to be familiar with the intricate details of Jewish dietary law unless you were raised in that tradition. (For hints on some religious no-nos, see "How to Pass with Class" #5.)

IN CASE OF EMERGENCY, PULL CORKSCREW

Dear Eve: *What should you do if you bring a really fine bottle of wine to a party and your hosts insist on serving plonk with dinner? Is it polite to ask for your own wine? N.S.*

It's not polite, but it may be necessary. A sensible host does not rely on guests bearing gifts to supply liquid accompaniment for a meal, and has ideally thought the matter of menu and tipple through. Traditionally, white wine goes with fish and red goes with dark meat. But who are you and I to argue that rotgut isn't the best thing to set off the gustatory pleasures of Chef Boy-ar-dee? *Chacun*'s *goût* is apparently not yours in this case.

I would recommend you grin and bear it — for the first bottle anyway. When uncorking time comes around again, which, with any luck, will be before your host serves the iceberg lettuce with bottled French dressing, you should clear your throat and venture: "Wouldn't you like to try some of the wine we brought? I first tasted it when I was visiting the south of France last summer and was delighted to discover when I got home that the local liquor store stocks it. Not many people are familiar with it, so I thought it would be nice to introduce my friends to it." It had better be good.

TOO FEW COOKS

I adore Indian food. I always keep a jar of mango pickles in the refrigerator for those inevitable days when one needs a hit of chili to unclog the sinuses and uncloud the brain. In a fit of ambition, I've undertaken mastering the art of the perfect chapatti. But the last time I tried to curry favor with my friends, the experience taught me a valuable lesson: gracious entertaining depends on having minions. Without a butler, a cook, an upstairs and a downstairs maid, it's virtually impossible to tend to guests' needs *and* keep an eye on the *saag bhaji*. So few people even have both an upstairs and a downstairs anymore, much less a maid for each. It is, therefore, absurd to consider serving anything more complicated than grilled lamb chops if the reason for having people over includes enjoying their company.

DEAR EVE: *I am a single man and I love to entertain. I have a lovely oak table which can seat ten comfortably but a tiny living room, so I naturally prefer sit-down dinners to buffet suppers. Yet, no matter how simple the menu I choose, I find myself dashing in and out of the kitchen all night long. Even though my guests offer to help, it often works out that having people running around makes things worse, not better. Can you suggest any ways of handling the problem? P.C.*

This is why potluck suppers will always be with us. If you insist on maintaining a certain standard, you'll have to compromise the Superman act; one does not preclude the other. I don't see why you can't organize your friends' willingness to be useful by delegating specific tasks in such a way that the helping hands will get less underfoot, so to speak. Just don't proceed on the assumption that all men are born knowing how to bartend and all women how to cook. One woman accepted a weekend invitation only to discover that her presence was primarily required in front of the stove. "She was a good cook as cooks go," Saki wrote, "and as good cooks go, she went."

It's preferable to conscript your guests ahead of time, giving each ample warning that there is a small price to be paid for the privilege of coming to dinner. When issuing invitations, ask one person to arrive a bit early to help you set the table, another to serve pre-dinner drinks.

Another possibility is to find a co-conspirator. There are companies which provide professional hostesses on the up-and-up for single businessmen who are required to entertain, and no doubt when their fees show up on expense reports, no one bats an eye. You probably will have to resort to amateurs, and in your circle there must be one friend you can trust to take coats and fix drinks while you concentrate on the pièce de résistance in the kitchen. His or her reward could be a dinner out on the town.

Simplify your service as much as possible. Plunk all the victuals down on the table at the same time and let everyone serve him or herself. If you must make soup, make it ahead of time and serve it cold. To my knowledge, no one has ever died of frostbite from eating iced cucumber soup in November. If you own a microwave oven, use it for all it's worth. If crêpes suzettes are the reason for your renown, have a crêpes suzettes party, and to hell with all the other fixings. Such niceties as sorbets between each of seven courses will have to be sacrificed to a greater cause: your being able to sit down and enjoy your own dinner. But the dishes, I'm afraid, are all yours to do.

SMOKE GETS IN MY EYES

DEAR EVE: *The time has come to take up the verbal cudgels against a group that is fast becoming the largest collection of boors since the Mongol hordes. I refer, of course, to reformed smokers who insist on waving their hands in front of people's faces or who say to near-strangers with a lit cigarette in their possession, "Would you mind putting that out?" It's time we "put them out" gracefully or taught them some manners.*

At my dinner parties, evangelists of any sort are not welcome. I agree that smoking is a filthy habit (so filthy, in fact, that I myself gave it up two years ago), but is it any worse than the habit of telling other people how to live? R.C.

Sigh. The whole issue of smoking etiquette is one that I try to avoid because I am a smoker myself, and my views are bound to be clouded over with the fumes of a freshly lit cigarette.

Fie on preachers of any ilk. Like you, I make a point of avoiding people whose idea of a good time is to inform me that brown rice is healthier than white, that jogging will improve my sex life and that I should sell my car as a protest against rising gas prices. In my innocence, I assume second-hand smoke is a nuisance on the level of cheap perfume and children who are trotted out to play the violin for guests, but non-smokers assure me it's a far greater aggravation.

A woman I know was forced for years to put up with a cantankerous relative who would ruin family occasions by lecturing Christmas or Thanksgiving visitors about their smoking. When she begged him to lay off, he announced he was allergic to cigarette smoke. Now there are people who really are allergic, and they should be shown every consideration. But his condition was suspiciously convenient.

The following Easter, my friend as usual planned a feast for family and friends. She called him up to tell him about it and said, "I'd really love to invite you but several of my guests are smokers, and I'd hate you to be uncomfortable." His allergy cleared up miraculously at the prospect of missing out on her ham.

ACCIDENTS DO HAPPEN

DEAR EVE: *I am the victimized host of a recent party. Everything was going smoothly when, to my horror, one of the guests broke her soup plate. She handed me the pieces without the slightest hint of an apology or offer of replacement. Of course, the dish was irreplaceable, a family heirloom passed down through four generations unscathed. Am I old-fashioned or was my guest rude? M.H.*

Come off it, Michael. You got that dish in Chinatown for $1.29. I would never have broken it if I hadn't choked on a shell in the oyster stew. And I *did* apologize — it was just hard to tell between the gasps.

But for the sake of argument, let's play this scene straight.

When you let strangers or even good friends into your home, you're running the risk they'll prove themselves to be utter barbarians, and by the time they're gone, you'll be grateful that at least the walls are still standing. Unless you're having the local motorcycle gang in for tea, however, I think it's safe to assume that any damage done in the course of a party is unintentional.

It pays to know that salt shaken on a red wine stain immediately after a glass is overturned will make the tablecloth easier to wash later on. Or that paper towels soaked in cold water are the best thing to wipe up coffee spilled on a white carpet. Most well brought-up guests will be mortified by spillage or breakage they have caused and will quickly volunteer to clean, wash, replace, etc. Or at least they should.

That means, yes, your guest was rude, but you don't have many options in the matter. If the dish was indeed irreplaceable, it's not going to do you much good to ask her to replace it. And if she's not the type to apologize on the spot, she's not the type to send you another dish or a bottle of wine or make any other gesture of apology. The only satisfaction you can get is to drop her from your guest list so that she can't do any more harm.

WHEN THE BELL RINGS, COME OUT FIGHTING

Dear Eve: *What happens if, at your dinner table, your guests start going at each other? I don't mean a physical fight — I'd feel obliged to break one up if it ever happened. But should a host step in and try to prevent people from engaging in verbal warfare? J.C.*

Bear with me — I'm going to answer this in a roundabout way.

Not too long ago, I found myself at an elegantly set table in one of the city's Better Neighborhoods. A most soignée soirée it was, and yours truly was doing her best not to discredit her punctilious profession. Using the proper fork and all that. However, the conversation soon took a turn for what proved to be the worse. My companion and I, being the only people present who might be considered, in relative terms, members of the younger generation, found ourselves defending the under-thirties in response to that perennially galling question, "What is wrong with kids today?" For every one of the other guests' repressive thrusts, we parried with a plea for permissiveness. Then, the old dope-versus-alcohol argument reared its head and, before anyone had time to react, one man rose swiftly from the table, beckoned to his wife, and they were out the front door in a flash of indignation. No thank-yous to the hostess, no good-nights in the direction of the company, no nothing. A pall descended over the Cointreau and coffee. Our host broke the puzzled silence by announcing: "I know what's eating him. His son has just been sentenced to a second term on drug charges."

I don't believe it is the duty of a host or hostess to protect guests from reality. It is one thing to request a special dish because one is allergic to certain foods, and quite another to insist that conversation be censored to prevent your discomfort.

I personally enjoy controversy; the most memorable parties I have attended have been ones where discussions were allowed to get at least passionate, if not downright ugly. I am aware, however, that such situations are only enjoyable if one does not have anything personally at stake in the subject matter.

There is, nonetheless, a difference between using discretion and using a muzzle. If you are at a gathering where you know that the mother of one of the other guests has just died of cancer and the conversation veers to a diatribe against the Cancer Society, you would be quite right to try to change the subject. But it would be only fair to the others to explain why you are doing so.

I found the precipitous exit of the unwittingly injured party that night to be insufferable. If you find yourself embarrassed, the least you owe others is not to embarrass them. Without necessarily making a clean breast of his particular problem, he should at least have said, "I'm sorry, but for reasons I'd rather not go into, I'd prefer it if we could change the subject." Anyone the least bit sensitive would have deferred to his wishes.

Being a host is not the same thing as being a referee. But if your guests start calling each other filthy names, perhaps it's time to clear your throat and say, "Come on, Jim. You're not playing fair." That's about as far as you should go. For all you know, you may be surprised, three days after the dinner, to receive a note in the mail which reads: "Thank you so much for the other evening. I really enjoyed meeting your friend Jim. It's so rare to get a chance to tackle an issue with someone who is not afraid to be opinionated. The food and wine were superb, as usual, but it was the adrenalin high which really made the party special for me."

A SIDE TRIP THROUGH THE SILVERWARE

When I set myself up in the social arbiter biz, I was determined not to concern myself with trivia such as table settings. But the first letters I received were about — you guessed it — and I was obliged to eat my words. With the proper cutlery, of course.

Knowing which knife and fork to use *is* important. Perhaps not as important as knowing whether gold is still a good investment or how to apply cardio-pulmonary resuscitation. But, as the nineteenth-century

American writer George Burgess pointed out, "Bad manners simply indicate that you care a good deal more for the food than the society at the table." And since most of us prefer dining with others to dining alone, it's important to pretend their presence counts. If you don't mind spending the rest of your life at a table for one, by all means skip this section. But if you do, the boundaries of boorishness at meals need to be chewed over from time to time.

You need never fear making a fool of yourself by picking up the wrong fork. Truly polite people make a point of ignoring the faux pas of others. A legendary Washington hostess once had a distinguished foreign ambassador as her guest. He ate the noodles in his soup with his fork. Rather than run the risk that he might be embarrassed by noticing he was alone in this practice, she did likewise.

Don't ever be daunted by a dazzling display of metal. It's very simple, really: the more knives and forks laid out, the more there will be to eat. Start with the utensils on the outside and work your way inward with each subsequent course. The fork and/or spoon above your plate is for dessert.

Everything you've heard about the butter knife is true. Never, ever transfer butter from the butter dish to the surface of your bread with the same gizmo. Instead, use the butter knife located near the butter dish to put a pat on your side plate, then go looking for your bread knife which, if you are at a very proper affair, should either be lying diagonally across your side plate or be the last one to your right in a row of knives.

If your hostess is not fortunate enough to own a complete service for twenty-two, she'll probably be tolerant enough to let you use the same knife to butter your bread, cut your meat and point at the fellow across the table during an argument. If she asks you to hang onto your flatware for the next course, do as she says. Put the fork with the tips of the tines facing down and rest the tip of your knife on the arc it forms so as to not dirty the tablecloth. (Finger-bowls on the table mean it's Tom Jones time, so tear into that artichoke, Cornish game hen or what-have-you without fear of opprobrium.) When you're through, line the fork and knife up together in the middle of the plate. I don't care what anyone says about tines up or tines down or ends pointing to the right or any of that stuff; as long as they aren't kicking around any which way ready to fall off the plate when it's lifted, you've done your bit to signal you've had your fill.

As for napkins, members of the family should roll cloth ones into napkin rings or fold them so that they can be reused, while guests crumple them up neatly and leave them where the plate used to be (or to the right, if it is still there) so that they can be sent immediately to the laundry. Paper ones may be left where they are (as long as it's not on the floor) or used for origami to amuse the other guests during coffee. Just don't make them into spitballs, that's all I ask.

And *c'est tout*. Unless you're eating Chinese or Japanese (feel free to fish things out of your soup with chopsticks and drink the liquid afterwards), Indian (it's *pukka* to tear off a piece of flatbread and use it to sop up the curry sauce) or in the company of Arabs (fingers of the right hand only, please — the left is considered unclean). You now know everything there is to know to eat anything anywhere at any time without ever appearing gauche. *Bon appétit.*

DEAR EVE: *Re the placement of silverware following a meal. Allow me to quote a passage from my oft-contemplated treatise, "A Waiter's Guide to Table Etiquette":*

Visualize the face of a clock on your plate. Now, the proper position for the knife and fork on the plate at the end of a meal is at four o'clock or, to be more accurate, at four twenty (a.m. or p.m. — I'm not that fussy).

As any waiter worth his salt knows, the correct way to serve food is from the diner's left. The correct way to remove a plate is from the right. Placing one's silverware properly enables the waiter to clamp his thumb firmly on the utensils, and thus ensures their safe removal. Consider it the ultimate insult when a waiter has to take the time to correctly position the silverware you have left all over the place.

Placing the utensils in this manner is a sure signal to the restaurant help that you have finished eating, in much the same way that closing the menu at the beginning of a meal is the correct way of letting a waiter know that you're ready to order. I learned all this in Home Economics class, or at my mother's knee, or somewhere. It was so long ago, I've forgotten. M.F.

One o'clock, two o'clock, three o'clock — fork. I think four o'clock is a perfectly ridiculous time to dine unless you're having tea at the Savoy.

I will admit your rule of (waiter's) thumb makes sense from a purely practical point of view. But does it really matter? As I've said before on the subject (and no doubt will say again), the proper criterion for the placement of a knife and fork when one has finished eating is neatness. If your utensils are stowed in such a way that they will not slide about when the plate is picked up, you've done your duty by the silverware. Please feel free to go right on doing it the way you always have.

DEAR EVE: *Before you close down on the cutlery question, please answer just one more query. This is to settle a debate that threatens the peace and quiet of a relatively peaceful group of relatives. Besides, I'd like some other topic of conversation. Here is what we need to know: when eating pie, tarts, puddings, etc. in the English fashion — spoon and fork — which hand holds the spoon and which the fork? The majority feels it's spoon right, fork left. Please let us know. E.K.*

Hmmm. Let's see ... you want to push with this ... then you want to bring it up to your mouth and then ... but you can cut better with a ... Okay, I think I've got it now. Take your cue from the way the utensils are laid out on the table. *The Amy Vanderbilt Complete Book of Etiquette* is so complete it even has pictures; you can check it out to see if you've been setting your table right all these years. If you hold the book right side up, you'll notice the spoon sits on top and faces west and the fork points east. For those of you who don't have a highly developed sense of direction, this means that, if you were to go for the spoon with your left hand and the fork with the right, you would wind up holding them by the bowl and the tines respectively. This is Not Done.

Faced with this overwhelming visual evidence, I'm forced to side with the spoon-right, fork-left contingent in your family squabble. The question, however, is not that simply resolved. There is the matter of *what* you eat with which one. Desserts of the viscous variety (pudding, fruit compotes, chocolate mousse, ice cream) may be eaten with a spoon only; you can use the fork in your left hand (tines facing down) to shovel the recalcitrant bits and pieces onto the spoon, but you're not obliged to. Likewise, solid sweets, such as cake, may be eaten with the fork only, if that's the way you feel most comfortable. You really need both when you have to tackle desserts that haven't made up their minds about consistency, such as trifle, mille-feuilles or crêpes with sticky things inside.

You can safely ignore all of the above when it comes to grapes (fingers will do). And never attend a dinner party where fresh, unpeeled mangoes are served. The only correct way to eat one of those is to lock yourself in the bathroom, get undressed, climb into the bathtub and go at it. Now — anyone care to discuss spaghetti?

CHAPTER SEVEN

Weddings

A well-planned wedding is like opening night on Broadway. It includes a great deal of preparation and nervousness on the part of the participants, a temperamental director (usually the mother of the bride), a producer who is panicky about exceeding the budget (usually the father of the bride) and two untried kids for whom it's a chance at the Big Time. But whether it's a gala performance with a cast of thousands or an intimate little production, it almost always turns out to be a great show, made all the more enjoyable for members of the audience by the fact that most of them are well acquainted with the stars.

For a long time, the few people left in this world who still found some validity in the institution of marriage were likely to clamber up hillsides barefoot at dawn or exchange their vows in mid-air during a parachute jump. I'm relieved to discover that those days are over, and the majority of people who have opted to marry rather than burn are willing to do it the old-fashioned way.

If you turned to this chapter hoping to find diagrams of who stands where in the receiving line, I'm sorry to disappoint you. The bridal how-to business has flourished in recent years, and far be it from me to devote my energies to arguing with the doyennes of decorum about the correct time to cut the cake. I can only recommend that anyone planning a major blow-out read Philip Roth's *Goodbye, Columbus* as a cautionary tale of excess before embarking on the project.

There have been a few wrinkles added to the whys and wherefores of marriage — most of them on the face of the bride and groom. People are getting married older than ever before. They are more experienced in the vicissitudes of life and love, and many have tried some variation of the theme on for size before they've actually said "I do."

I TAKE THEE ... AND THE TOASTERS AND THE TOWELS

DEAR EVE: *A friend is getting married and has placed her name with a bridal registry. What exactly is this and how does it operate? E.L.*

A bridal registry is either a great convenience or ritualized conspicuous consumption, depending on your attitude to gadgets. I'll try not to let my prejudices show too much.

Since a couple cannot possibly embark upon married life without the appropriate accessories (china, flatware, convection ovens, electric bun warmers), and since they would rather spend the first few weeks of wedded bliss doing something other than returning three identical (and utterly useless) silver platters, the bride-to-be can spare herself untold aggravation by letting her guests know precisely what is expected of them. It would be *déclassé* to inform everyone personally of the desirability of Waterford goblets, so a department store provides the useful service of acting as a discreet middleman.

It goes something like this: the bride visits the store and, with the help of far too much solicitous advice from a "bridal consultant" ("Well, maybe you're right ... the Royal Doulton china would look better with slightly less contemporary stemware ..."), checks her preferences off on a registry sheet. She then lets the word out that a certain emporium has in stock everything her little heart desires. One bridal consultant I consulted in the course of duty tsk-tsks the notion of including the name of the store with the invitation. I concur wholeheartedly and regret that some lesser enterprises might recommend it on grounds of convenience (theirs, no doubt).

You, as the guest, may avail yourself of this service by phoning or visiting the store and inquiring what on the bride's checklist has not already been purchased. If you discover she needs only one more place setting to complete a service for fifty-seven or that the sterling silver nutpicks are within your price range, you need look no further.

The one great advantage of bridal registries is for those who live outside the couple's home city. When a bride registers with a store that's part of a chain, her list is photocopied and sent to all branches. Her guests (even those who will not be able to attend the wedding) can thus pay for an item in their city and the order will be filled and delivered in another (ideally, where the wedding is taking place).

You are by no means restricted to the bill of goods at the registree's choice of shops. If you promised the couple to blow up and frame that photo you took of them skinny-dipping in the lake last summer, the fact that it doesn't come in a box bearing a company logo will not diminish its value.

DEAR EVE: *We have been living together for four years and have decided to get married. Our original plans were for a simple gathering of friends, but now that everyone from relatives to co-workers have put in their two cents' worth, we find ourselves with a three-ring circus on our hands. We fought it off as best we could but finally decided (since our respective mothers were having such a ball arranging the whole thing) we might as well enjoy it.*

Our problem is this: we have everything we need in the way of towels, pots and pans and household appliances, yet uncles and aunts and assorted well-wishers insist on carrying out the charade that we're sweet young things setting up housekeeping for the first time. I don't wish to sound too mercenary about it, but is there any way to avoid having to return four toasters to the store? V.R.

It is, as you so accurately point out, a charade, but a lovely and enjoyable one for many people, the bride and groom being the least of them. I've always held that love is a private matter between two people, but a wedding is an interchange between the couple on the one hand and the world at large on the other. By getting married, you are going public with your affection for, and your commitment to each other.

The audience's traditional response to a wedding is not applause but presents. (I have heard of one ceremony after which the congregants clapped, but that wasn't a wedding, it was a corporate merger.) While it is a refreshing change to hear from someone who is *not* getting married merely to round out a collection of Le Creuset cookware, I'm sorry to report that there's very little you can do. When it comes to wedding gifts, toasters and their ilk are it. Friends of mine found themselves in a similar situation. When the bride-to-be was asked where she was registered, she replied, only half facetiously, "The Chase Manhattan Bank." For all that, the last time I saw her, she was balefully staring down an unnecessary and unwelcome Cuisinart on her kitchen counter.

You really only have two choices in this matter: you either request that no gifts be given at all or you graciously accept the ones that are. What you do with the gifts once you have them is between you and your conscience. Look, we're dealing with tradition here. You may not be sweet young things setting up house for the first time, but if the bride is planning to wear white ... need I say more?

DEAR EVE: *Could you suggest some appropriate wedding gifts for two people who are both getting married a second time and have all the goods they need? Should any consideration be given to the possibility that this marriage too might not make it, and that they might have to split the gifts up? I thought of giving them six glasses so they could each have three if worse comes to worst. P.W.*

The world is full of cynics. One of them, Samuel Johnson, is famous for having described second marriages as "the triumph of hope over experience." Another one, a contemporary of mine, has vowed to give all the second-time-arounders used toasters. Pay them no never mind.

I, for one, would like to see hope triumph for a change. Forget the easily splittable gifts and give from the heart. You're right that things may not be needed, although there's nothing wrong with decorative knick-knacks or artwork if you know their tastes. More appreciated gifts might be food for thought or R and R. I suggest a subscription to their favorite magazine, a year's home delivery of the morning paper, dinner for two at a fine restaurant, or a night's stay at a good hotel so that they can have some sort of honeymoon in town if they can't get away. Or volunteer to babysit children from previous marriages so that they can spend some time alone. Or any combination of the above, if you can afford it.

I once offered a bride-to-be a professional massage on the

morning of the wedding. These gifts can't be held and looked at down the road, or divided evenly, but they will be remembered.

DEAR EVE: *I would like to give a young couple about to be married a cheque as a gift. Could you please let me know to whom the cheque should be made payable? M.H.*

Make it out to the person you know best. If it's the bride, make it payable to her under her maiden name. Address the envelope with both their names and enclose a little note saying, "This is for both of you to enjoy." Many women keep their own names these days, and you can't possibly be expected to know whether they have a joint chequing account at the bank.

DEAR EVE: *We were invited to a wedding and sent along a present. Two days before the ceremony was to take place, we received a notice in the mail saying the wedding had been called off. Would it be tacky to write and ask for our present back? P.W.*

Incredibly tacky. Tremendously tacky. Tacky, tacky, tacky. The mind reels at the tackiness of it all. I need a drink, a Valium ... something, quick. Oh, thank heavens ... that's much better. Now, where were we?

Do not, under any circumstances, write and ask for your present back. Don't you think these people have enough on their minds? They'll need some time to recover from the shock of not tying the knot and having to explain it all to their friends to boot. Allow for a respectable period of fainting spells on the part of prospective mothers-in-law, not to mention the florist and the caterer. Once things calm down, your present should be returned entirely unsolicited. If it isn't, your friends are tacky.

MEMBERS OF THE WEDDING

DEAR EVE: *I am getting married in December and my fiancé and I have chosen to go with a fairly formal ceremony. The problem is that my mother is a widow, so there will be no father-of-the-bride to give me away. What are my options in this situation? T.W.*

Unlimited. The notion of a bride as chattel goods being handed over from one "owner" to another has been, the saints be praised, washed up on shore by the tide of feminism. It is included in some ceremonies as a bow to tradition and, along with the best man's role as defender of the groom and the "first" night at the motel, is one of The Things We Do But Don't Really Believe. I'm all for tradition, as long as we don't lose sight of its symbolic nature.

Call a meeting with your mother, your fiancé and the priest, minister or rabbi to decide on something you all can live with. Your mother has a right to give you away if she chooses; in that case, she should wait for you at the altar while a brother or other male relative marches you up the aisle. Or a male relative can do the job by stating at the appropriate moment, "In her mother's name, I do."

You might want to consider doing it yourself (Officiant: "Who gives this woman in marriage?" Bride: "I give myself freely"). You could even pass up that part of the ceremony altogether if none of these alternatives suit your tastes. As long as the proper papers are signed, your marriage will be legal, whatever you choose to do.

DEAR EVE: *I am going to be best man at a friend's wedding. I've got the routine pretty well under control — the ring, boutonnieres and all that. But I keep hearing a lot of loose talk among all our male friends about the great stag they're looking forward to, and every time the subject comes up, they all look at me expectantly. Is this part of my duties as well? If so, how do I go about organizing one? D.C.*

Never having been baked inside a cake — the only acceptable way, it seems, for someone of my gender to attend a stag — I can't say I have much first-hand experience in these matters. But I do have male friends who have been beneficiaries (or victims, depending on your point of view) of this grand old chauvinistic tradition and who are willing to tell all.

The idea behind a stag is that it is the groom's big chance to get every last bit of philandering out of his system. There's an old Limelighters' song that has become something of an anthem for the occasion:

One more poor lamb to slaughter led
We doff our hats and wave good-bye
No longer shall he join the chase
Or ever cast a roving eye.

A likely story. But such are the myths of male camaraderie.

The onus for organizing this affair does not rest entirely on your shoulders: the stag is one duty shared by the best man and the ushers. Before you go all out, make sure that your efforts will be appreciated. Not every groom relishes the notion of sitting around just before his wedding getting sloshed with his pals.

If you get the go-ahead, you'll need to rent a hotel room or arrange for the use of someone's home and stock up on lots of liquor and chips, both potato and poker. Gambling is the prime activity of the night and not just as another way of flouting conventional morality. In the old days, one of the purposes of the stag was to raise money for the groom to allow him to embark on married life with a bit of loose change in his pocket. His friends would contribute a percentage of the pot so that he could continue to drink with them after his bride had taken control of the household finances. That's all very well and good for a seventeen-year-old Shropshire farm hand, but it doesn't make much sense if you're a thirty-five-year-old corporate executive.

I won't presume to advise you on ecdysiasts, X-rated films and Extra Old Stock. I know they're all considered prime ingredients of a successful stag, but they're areas in which I am, for once, willing to concede the superiority of male knowledge.

DEAR EVE: *I have been asked to be toastmaster at my niece's wedding. I would be pleased if you could inform me of what is expected of me in this role. G.J.H.*

If you approach the task as an honor instead of as a duty, you might even enjoy yourself. No one is more popular than the person who has nothing but good to say about someone else, and that is what your niece is counting on you to do.

You probably know the bride and her parents relatively well, but you should also take time before the wedding day to find out some personal details about the groom and his family. On the big day, your job begins after all the guests have finished eating. Get everyone's attention by tapping lightly on your wine glass with a spoon. (It is the caterer's responsibility to make sure that the wine glasses are filled.) Lead off with a few general remarks about the happiness of the event and how pleasant it is to have everyone present to share in the celebration. Toast the bride first by raising your glass in her direction and making a few intimate but non-condescending remarks.

"I remember the day you helped us paint the kitchen. You looked as beautiful in paint-splattered overalls as you do in your bridal gown" is good. "I bet you're glad your parents paid to have your teeth straightened" is not; there's one too many Don Rickles in this world as it stands. Take a small sip of wine (or fake it if you wish to remain clear-headed), wait for the company to follow your example, then turn your attention to the bride's parents. Repeat the formula for them, the groom, the groom's parents and the officiating priest, minister or rabbi in that order. You may then read congratulatory telegrams, signal the orchestra to start playing and wind up your remarks by announcing, "Let the dancing begin!" If everyone doesn't think you're a swell guy after all that, I'll eat my white gloves.

DEAR EVE: *I've been a toastmaster at a wedding several times and I've been required to read telegrams as part of my job. Some of the telegrams were really tasteless, "joke" type things that none of the other guests seemed to appreciate either. Is it okay to just slip these in your pocket and ignore them, or are you obliged to read them anyway? G.L.*

If your friends take their wedding seriously, you should too. A reception is not a cabaret, and your purpose is not to amuse the assembled company but to make sure everyone has a good time. Parents should be spared innuendos about their son's or daughter's sexual past, and the minister should not have to listen to language he would never include in a sermon himself. A toastmaster has every right to exercise his judgment as part of his function. By all means show the "jokes" to the bride and groom in private, but as far as the public is concerned: when in doubt, leave it out.

DEAR EVE: *A friend of mine is getting married for the second time. She has, to my delight, asked me to be her bridesmaid. I know she and her husband-to-be are paying for the whole celebration. In other words, there are no parents footing the bill for a lavish ceremony. In a situation like this, who is supposed to pay for my dress? D.C.*

I'm afraid you are. You're a big girl now, and you have to buy your own clothes. Even at a first wedding, bridal attendants cannot take anything for granted. A bride (or rather her family) traditionally pays for her entourage's flowers at the very least and offers some token of appreciation for taking part, which sometimes is in the form of assuming the cost of their clothing. If the bride is going to be upset to find she is not flanked by six matching pairs of gold lamé pyjamas by Valentino at the altar, she damn well better be prepared to pay the freight. But otherwise, expenses such as outfitting the participants are to be negotiated between those who are paying and those who are participating. For example, the groom might buy gloves and ties for his ushers; the bride might buy her bridesmaids' dresses; the groom's family might underwrite hotel accommodation and travel costs for their out-of-town members of the wedding and the bride's family for theirs. But all these things are optional and should be agreed upon before anyone finds him or herself unduly out of pocket.

For a second wedding, you can safely disregard all of the above, regardless of whether there are any parents footing the bill. It is not traditional for a second-time bride to wear white and stage a production worthy of Cecil B. De Mille. She usually doesn't have more than one or two attendants, and the fact that their satin pumps aren't dyed to the exact same shade of cerise should not interfere with the proceedings. But do check with her about your planned ensemble so that the two of you don't wind up next to each other in clashing shades of orange.

If you don't own a comfortable, dressy number which would be suitable for a wedding, why not view this as the perfect excuse to buy one? You would be sensible to get something you could recycle for cocktail parties and other ceremonies of life.

THE GUEST LIST

I'm still romantic enough to believe a wedding should be for the benefit of the bride and groom, and that all of Daddy's debtors and creditors have no business being there. Of course Aunt Flossie should be prevailed upon to leave her rosebushes in peace for one day and make the journey into town, but a guest list is not the same as a Christmas card list.

DEAR EVE: *I have been invited to a formal wedding. The invitation was addressed only to me, but there is a woman I have been seeing a lot of recently and I was wondering if it would be okay to bring her? D.E.*

Certainly not. There are the practical aspects to be considered, such as the disruption of carefully thought-out seating plans. If the invitation did not allow for another body either by name or in general (as in "Mr. Robert Jones and Companion") there will simply not be room for her at any of the tables.

DEAR EVE: *I used to date a married man for whom I still care a great deal. I'm getting married myself and I would like him to attend the wedding. My problem is: can I get away with sending an invitation just to him and not also to his dear wife? Believe me, her blessings are not welcome, and she can dance at someone else's nuptials. P.R.*

If you try to pull a stunt like this, she'll be dancing on your grave, not at your wedding. I assume you and your former lover are quite practised in the art of deception; you'll have to resort to it again, I'm afraid. A verbal invitation would be preferable to a written one — it can't be used as evidence in divorce court. It will be up to him to cover his tracks on the day of the festivities and up to you to explain his presence to your new husband.

Perhaps you'll consider marching down the aisle to "Your Cheating Heart" instead of "Here Comes the Bride"? As you may have gathered, I don't approve.

FOR RICHER OR FOR POORER

DEAR EVE: *I am planning a summer wedding. My parents cannot contribute too much to the cause since their means are limited, but my fiancé and I would like to invite about two hundred people. He has found a nice little vegetarian restaurant in the country, about thirty miles out of town, which will give us a good deal. But my aunt, who is considerably better off than any of us, has offered us the use of a country club to which she belongs. It is much closer to town where most of our guests live and I would much prefer it. I'm afraid of hurting his feelings. C.M.*

The bride and her family usually choose the spot for the reception. I'm sure that not all of your guests will be trendy young things delighted at the prospect of trekking out into the country in search of wholesomeness. The guest list will probably also include arthritic grandmothers and paunchy uncles who are accustomed to Swedish meatballs and comfort on such occasions.

I would accept your aunt's generous offer, but I would append certain conditions (such as choosing the menu and arranging the seating yourselves) to appease your fiancé. Nothing is more welcome than a gift one couldn't afford otherwise.

DEAR EVE: *My girlfriend and I moved to the city some time ago. After years of putting it off, we finally decided to Do the Right Thing and get married. Since both of our families are still in our home town and we've kept up our friendships with people there, we chose it as the venue for the ceremony and reception.*

When we came back to the city, our friends here started asking us when we planned to have a reception they could attend. Frankly, we hadn't planned on another one, but it's true that it would be nice to celebrate with our new friends as well as the old. We can't really afford to have another big bash. Are we obliged to do it again? H.K.

No one is obliged to do anything at all when they get married. The bride may wear purple, the groom an old T-shirt and running shoes, and the ceremony may be performed in the middle of an intersection, as long as it doesn't impede traffic. Most people don't go to those extremes of non-conformity because of peer pressure. Your peers, however, are pressuring you a bit too much.

If your friends are so desperate to celebrate your nuptials, why don't they throw a party for you? I think it's a bit unfair of them to expect you to spend any more money than you already have, what with travelling home and organizing a fête there. If they can't get it together, tell them you plan to celebrate your first anniversary with them if they'll just hold on a bit longer.

CHAPTER EIGHT

Babies

A writer and a photographer huddle intently over a cup of coffee at a chic downtown café. What can they be discussing? The fascistic quality of Helmut Newton's work? The decline of Susan Sontag as the ranking essayist of popular culture? No, no, my dears. She's wondering if she should start weaning her baby daughter and he's concerned that his infant son's colic has been caused by an allergy to cow's milk. They cover all the bases of parenthood, including the advantages of Pampers over cloth diapers.

Eavesdropping just ain't what it used to be. I used to take a great delight in keeping one ear constantly cocked for what might prove to be human drama unfolding. But of late, there seems to be only one act, and it's ferociously boring: babies. Babies and babies. Babies and more babies. The infamous postwar baby boom has taken to reproduction with a vengeance. Call your dearest friends on the phone and ask them what's new at your peril. "The ultrasound was positive, and we're going to the hospital next weekend for a look at the birthing room." Enough!

Everyone, but *everyone* I know is reproducing like mad. There seem to be as many birth announcements in the mail as there are bills. I remarked upon this to friends who had brought their heir apparent around for a viewing and muttered something along the line of "I don't know what it is. It must be in the wind." The proud father threw back his shoulders and laughed, "Actually, there's a bit more contact involved."

Not so long ago, when a woman friend phoned to announce she was pregnant, one didn't know whether to congratulate or commiserate. Now that I can't find company to go to the movies with because they're all attending pre-natal classes, it's pretty clear they're doing it on purpose.

IS SHE OR ISN'T SHE?

DEAR EVE: *One of the women in our office is looking considerably more ample in girth than usual. She's wearing billowy dresses and loose shirts all of a sudden. Can we safely assume she is advertising her pregnancy? Is there any discreet way of asking? E.T.*

If she is pregnant, I'm sure she's not sporting a new wardrobe merely to communicate her condition to her co-workers; an office memo would be more to the point. But yes, you can safely assume she is, especially if she's also smiling a lot (a newly fat person wouldn't look so pleased with herself, jolly stereotypes to the contrary).

Most women do announce their pregnancy officially at some point, even if it's only to the people in the office to whom they feel close, or to the boss to give fair warning about possible maternity leave. If you're shy about approaching your colleague directly, a bit of judicious snooping would probably satisfy your curiosity.

If you do get confirmation from someone in the know, it would be quite all right to congratulate her. And, for heaven's sake, don't be shy about calling things by their proper names. A colleague of mine, when she was seven months along, was amused and amazed by the variety of euphemisms people resorted to when they were trying to hedge their bets: Is your family expanding? Is there a wee one on the way? Are you with child? Looking forward to a blessed event? In the family way? They're all perfectly charming and all perfectly unnecessary.

TOO CLOSE FOR COMFORT

DEAR EVE: *I am six months pregnant. People offer me their seats on the subway and smile at me a lot. Com-*

plete strangers come up to me and ask when the baby is due. I must admit I am enjoying it. Except for one thing: sometimes they go too far. In the last week, at least six people have patted me on the stomach. I know they mean well, but I don't like being pawed. How can I get them to stop? P.L.B.

In your condition, you are no longer a person, you are a monument to motherhood. People can't resist making contact. I suspect it's rather like kissing the Blarney Stone or wearing down the pillars of the Parthenon with an awe-inspired touch.

From where you sit, of course, you are still a sentient human being, and what they're doing is not unlike pinching your bottom or placing an unsolicited hand on your breast, dubiously friendly gestures at best. You could always try to duck the offending, if well-intentioned hand, but it's better to try stopping it in its tracks. Grab it on its trajectory, give it an affectionate squeeze and say: "Appearances to the contrary, I am not the Laughing Buddha."

SHOWERED WITH AFFECTION

DEAR EVE: *A friend of mine is having a baby. I don't know any of her co-workers or her other friends (I know her through her husband, who is a co-worker of mine, but we do socialize once or twice a month). Am I required to give a shower or attend any? Frankly, they are not my idea of a good time and neither is looking for baby accessories. I'd rather get her something else, but it seems that nothing is good for pregnant women except pregnancy. G.D.*

Such tenuous connections do not carry with them any obligations. Friendship, unlike family, is still the domain of voluntary acts of kindness. Since you don't know any of her co-workers or friends, you would be hard-pressed to know whom to invite, so keep the punch bowl in the cupboard for an event that is liable to be better attended. Her co-workers and friends are probably as blissfully unaware of your existence as you are of theirs, so the likelihood of being summoned to a shower arranged by the folks at her office is slim. No sense worrying about turning down invitations you are not likely to receive.

Let the shower-goers and relatives worry about outfitting the latest messiah. If your imagination, like mine, does not extend beyond stuffed toys as a way of greeting newcomers to the planet, wait till the kid is old enough to have a sensible conversation about what it can use to make its way in the world.

In the meantime, concentrating on Mom is a splendid idea; in all the excitement over the outcome of her labors, she tends to be forgotten. A lacy nightgown to remind her of the urge that was responsible for all this would surely bring a smile to her face, not to mention the father's. A bouquet of flowers sent (or even better, delivered personally) to the hospital is always a class act. And if you want to give her the one gift for which she will be eternally grateful, stick an IOU for an evening of babysitting in among the roses. Time for herself is a present any new mother can use.

DEAR EVE: *I am expecting my first baby and therefore also my first baby shower. Friends keep asking me what I think I'll need and I tell them quite frankly. My parents live far away, and I'm coming to the realization that cribs, clothes, diaper pails and car seats are going to be a great expense, so we could use all the help we can get. I thought of drawing up a list of must-have items and circulating it among my friends. Do you think this would be impolite? M.O.*

Baby showers (and wedding showers and housewarmings) exist primarily for the purpose of easing our friends' financial burdens, and I'm all for them. Toasters for people who have lived together for decades are silly, I grant you, but the idea of helping out is a noble one.

For some time now, department stores and boutiques, with their bridal registries, have been quite happily cashing in on people's desire to give newlyweds what they really want. I have not heard of baby registries but maybe they're due. All that registries of any sort do is act as middlemen. I see no reason why you couldn't borrow their modus operandi.

I suggest you enlist the aid of a close friend, perhaps the person you feel is most likely to throw the shower for you. If you were to simply send a list of your needs to your friends at large, they might take it the wrong way. But if you give the list to one person and say, "If people ask you what you think they should get for the baby, this might give you some ideas of what to tell them," you will appear considerably less greedy. Your friend will thus become a sort of baby registry on your behalf, people will know what you want and, with any luck, you'll get what you need.

Dear Eve: *My husband has been just super throughout my pregnancy, so much so that I really don't feel I am alone in this. He has been taking prenatal classes with me, he's planning to be in the delivery room, and if ever a baby was a joint effort, I feel this one will be. The problem is that some friends are planning to throw a shower for me, and my husband wants to come along. He wasn't specifically invited, and my mother thinks it would be improper for him to attend. What do you think? W.L.*

Oh, balderdash. It's his baby too, isn't it? Your mother may have had to bear the weight of womanhood alone, but unfortunate experiences do not define propriety. If your mother doesn't deem it correct for him to cross the boundaries into a "woman's world" by going to a baby shower, I shudder to think how she feels about his being part of the proceedings on D-day, or how she'll react to the first sight of him with a diaper pin between his teeth.

The only reservation I have about his attending the shower is that he might be embarrassed by the cloying sentimentality usually expressed on such occasions. My experience of them is of grown women giggling and going gaga over eensy-weensy 'ittle jammies and Pooh-Bear diaper pails. If he's man enough not to succumb to an overdose of terminal cuteness, I say let him go.

Dear Eve: *Are you obliged to bring a present to a christening? I sent one after the baby was born and need to know if I have to get another for this occasion. R.M.*

No. A christening usually takes place some time after the happy event and is one of the few festivities that is still primarily religious. You've done your bit by the bairn.

AN OFFER HE CAN'T REFUSE

Dear Eve: *A friend of mine has asked me to be the godfather of his son. I said "yes" right away and only later realized that I don't really know what sort of a responsibility that is. Could you please tell me what exactly it entails? P.A.*

No doubt you have already gathered it has nothing to do with strolling down the street on a Sunday morning wearing your best black pin-striped suit and waving your diamond-studded pinky ring at well-wishers. However, it does mean your friend thinks highly of you, thinks you are trustworthy and wants to involve you in one of the most significant events of his life.

Being a godfather used to mean being responsible for the child's religious education, but that is less and less the case. The vestiges of the tradition remain in that the godparents attend the child's christening and perform roughly the same functions as a best man and matron of honor at a wedding — in other words, they hover about and try to be as useful as possible.

Being a godparent also used to mean there would always be someone to look after the child should he or she be orphaned. This function has been taken over by various social agencies, but the implication remains that you are morally responsible for the child's well-being.

The one tradition still observed is that of presenting the child with a token of your special relationship. A teddy bear is not enough; it must be something the child will have all his life to remind him you are part of it. Gold or silver is usually called for. Give him either a gold pinky ring with his initials (so he can wave it at well-wishers when he grows up) or a small silver monogrammed mug. Money is always nice; in the form of a savings bond it would be most practical. You don't have to give the parents anything beyond proof that you are worthy of their trust.

THROUGH THICK AND THIN

Dear Eve: *A group of us is very upset. A couple we are all friends with announced they were going to have a baby about a year ago, and nobody's heard from them since about two months before the wife was due to deliver. Everybody is assuming something went wrong, but we're all scared to call and find out in case it's true. What should we do? C.G.*

Call, dammit. Friendship isn't all fun and games — it's also being there for the rough times. It does seem that something's not right, which is all the more reason that you should make yourselves available. But don't go galumphing in with flowers and sympathy cards until you know exactly what has happened.

One of you should phone and make inquiries with the most tact you can muster. A simple "Hello. Haven't heard from you for a while. How are things?" will allow them to give you the good or bad news on their own terms. If it's bad news, let them define the sort of help they need, if any, and be prepared to follow through.

FEEDING TIME

DEAR EVE: *I am a nursing mother and circumstances often demand that I feed my infant son in public. I don't really mind since my baby's hunger is more important than my modesty, but my problem is what to do with my nursing shields while I feed the baby. I have tried slipping the shield into my hand and then concealing it in the folds of my skirt, but invariably I forget about it, get up and walk off, leaving it behind on my chair. It is very embarrassing. What can I do? E.C.*

Discretion is the better part of breastfeeding, as it is of so many other things. Your letter suggests you are quite above the controversy of whether nursing in public is polite in the first place, and I must admit I am firmly on your side in this. It is only in our so-called civilized society that the sight of a mother nurturing her young is repugnant. I'm sure we shall get over it the way we eventually got over putting frilly pantaloons on the "limbs" of furniture.

The La Leche League, an international organization formed to promote breast-feeding, recommends that you not make an overt display of the process. I applaud your attitude if you define "public" as the homes of friends or even small gatherings of people you know well. I just trust you are not indulging in the practice on the down escalator of a department store or in Row R on opening night at the theater. Should you find yourself in such circumstances, retreat to the nearest public washroom and fulfill your obligation there. In all cases, keep in mind that you will be thought less of a nuisance if you withdraw to as private a corner as possible to attend to your son's needs than if you allow him to scream his lungs out in frustration.

If you persist in leaving bits of apparatus around, you are playing into the hands of those who frown on breastfeeding in the first place. They're hard enough to ignore as it is, so do try to be neater. I asked a member of La Leche about your problem since she has infinitely more experience than I do in such matters.

She advises that you shouldn't be using store-bought shields in the first place; they tend to be made of plastic materials and don't allow your skin to breathe. A small square of terry towelling will protect your clothes just as well. When the moment comes to bare your breast, simply tuck the cloth into the side of your bra, out of the way for your purposes but still firmly in place in the interests of decorum. It may not be as elegant as a fine linen handkerchief, but no one will suspect otherwise if you act as though it is.

THE POSTPARTUM BLUES

New mothers aren't the only ones who get depressed when all the fuss is over.

DEAR EVE: *What do you do when you want to spend time with a girlfriend who insists on bringing her baby on every outing? How can you tactfully ask her to leave the kid behind? J.W.*

Sounds like maternal bonding is coming between you and a good time. First of all, you have to accept that friendships, no matter how close, must inevitably be redefined when something happens to one of you that hasn't happened to the other. Falling in love, getting married and starting a family are three of the deadliest enemies of buddyhood. To you, the fact that she's had a kid is old news already, so let's get on with it. To her, the center of the universe has just shifted 180 degrees.

If she has just had the baby, and especially if she's breastfeeding, your chances of prying the two of them apart are about nil. You either hang in and enjoy the madonna routine, or you find yourself another bumming around pal for the interim.

However, if she's been up to her elbows in soiled diapers for a while, some of the thrill is certainly gone, and she'd probably welcome the opportunity of temporary escape. Wait till you hear her sigh about the responsibilities of motherhood and jump right in with: "I bet you could really use a break from time to time. I've got a great idea — why don't the two of us take an afternoon off together, do a bit of shopping, have some tea or catch a movie? I'll find you a baby-sitter if Nick can't stay home to look after Junior that day." What are friends for?

DEAR EVE: *What do you say if you go over to visit friends who have just had a baby and the baby is perfectly hideous? D.B.S.*

Lie. They no doubt think the child is magnificent; so who are you to shatter their illusions? After all the work they did, even if it was to produce something less than the Ivory Snow baby, they have the right to expect a little oohing and aahing in appreciation. The orthodontist's bill doesn't arrive until much later. Simply turn to the parent you like least, smile sincerely and say, "Congratulations. He looks just like you."

DEAR EVE: *Friends recently brought their baby to a dinner party of mine and, as a result, all conversation focused on the baby. I've invited them again, but don't know how to let them know I'd rather they came sans child. Any ideas? S.M.*

It may be too late. The best way I can think of doing it is to say at the moment of invitation, "I'm planning a dinner on Friday night and I'd love to have you come. Do you think you'll be able to get a sitter that evening?"

CHAPTER NINE

As My First Wife Used to Say

We're far too civilized about breaking up. We've swallowed whole the notion that yelling, screaming and bawling our little hearts out is childish and undignified. It is considered much more mature to pop a tranquilizer, which is why, I'm convinced, the pharmaceutical companies are flourishing. Where are "the vapors" now that we need them? Whatever happened to six months on the Continent to mend a broken heart? Duels at daybreak?

We've conned ourselves into thinking that the "adult" thing to do is to make the transition from six years' worth of daily intimacy to casual dinners once a month without missing a beat. People who used to be the best of lovers are now proclaiming they're the best of friends, and they expect those in their social circle to accept the metamorphosis without batting an eye. Who is fooling whom, may I ask?

I am willing to be the first in my crowd to admit I go completely around the bend when a relationship fails. Having several times in recent years been put together again by all the king's horses and all the king's men (not to mention friends, Krazy Glue and a couple of bottles of Laphroaig's finest single malt), I must warn you that I am outrageously biased on the subject of the splits.

Picking up the pieces at the end of a long-term commitment is never pleasant or easy. The matter is endlessly complicated by the wide variety of guises in which The End manifests itself. It may be as simple as a live-in couple's decision that one of them (and the canary) has to go, or as overwrought as an interminable suit over division of property after a divorce. Widowhood is no longer the only way out.

But whether singledom comes in on little cat's feet or a relationship ends with a bang, life goes on. The more often one goes through it, the more often one comes to the conclusion that there's no getting away from clichés.

***Dear Eve:** My divorce will soon be final. I had the idea to celebrate (the marriage was really bad), but I'm afraid this would be considered tasteless. What do you think? M.P.*

Emily Post will no doubt be spinning in her grave, but I think it's a marvelous idea. We mark every other milestone in our lives, and I find it a shame we have thus far failed to ritualize this particular one. The purpose of ceremonies, or rites of passage, is to publicly acknowledge a change of status — from boy to man, from student to scholar, from pagan to Christian, from one to two. You were a married woman and now you're not; if it gives you cheer, it's something to share with the world.

Charlotte Ford, very up-to-date in her *Book of Modern Manners*, reports that the United Methodist Church looks kindly on such ceremonies and offers a sample text for those who wish the blessings of a priest or rabbi in the rending of their union. It's a bit high-toned for my tastes (sample question by officiant: "Matthew Surrey, do you now relinquish your status as husband of Anne, freeing her from all claims upon and responsibilities to you except those you willingly give to all other children of God?"), but I can appreciate that it gives comfort to those who are spiritually inclined.

I myself would prefer a raucous gathering, more in the tradition of an Irish wake, with much music, laughter and drinking of champagne. If you've never been a debutante, consider this your coming out party.

However, I am still of two minds on a related issue: making the divorce public beyond informing your immediate circle of friends. I hear rumors that there now exists on the market a delightful thing known as a divorce announcement card.

It goes something like:

Mr. and Mrs. Simon Kneff
are pleased to inform you
of the impending dissolution of their
marriage.
The decree nisi has been arranged
(on amicable terms)
by Mr. David Bartholomew
of Bartholomew, Bartholomew and Bartholomew
and
Mr. Sylvester Stein
of Stein, Stein and Bartholomew.
The decree absolute will follow.

By all means, send one to your friends for a giggle. But spare your parents, maiden aunts, minister, boss, professional associates and anyone else who might find the matter of divorce less than a laughing matter. It's amusing all right, but it will never have the social cachet of a wedding invitation. At least not if I have anything to say about it.

YOU CAN HAVE TED, BUT I'LL KEEP SUSAN

DEAR EVE: *My wife and I split up about three months ago. Our present relationship is amicable if a bit cool. The problem is that during the seven years we were together, I got very close to her parents. My own family was never what you'd call tightly knit, but I got along really well with both her father and her mother.*

We didn't see too much of each other after the divorce, but her mother's birthday is coming up and I thought of sending her a card or something in the hope that it might help to re-establish contact. Do you think it's the right thing to do? G.J.

Absolutely. I don't guarantee that you will automatically be welcomed back into the fold, but at least this way they will know that the channels of communication are still open, and they can take the next step.

No two people I've ever heard of sit down after a break-up and try to divide up their human assets as well as their chattel goods in an equitable manner. ("You can have the ship's clock and Susan, I'll take the Chindia rug and Ted.")

Obviously, her claim to her parents is more immediate than yours but that doesn't mean you have no rights at all. They may no longer be your in-laws, but they may very well still be your friends as long as you give them no cause to feel their loyalties are divided. Don't use your friendship as a message service between you and your ex, and don't rely on them as a sounding board for all your grievances against her.

They may have kept their distance out of respect for what they considered to be your wishes, or they may not have wanted to appear to be meddling. If you send out a signal that the way is clear again, I see no reason why a redefined friendship could not be resumed.

DEAR EVE: *When my marriage ended, my husband and I, still on good terms, entered an awkward period over the division of friends. Recently, a couple who had befriended us both invited only me to a party. I know if my former husband hears about it he will be very upset. Do I invite him along as my date anyway? Or do I simply weather the inevitable tripe to follow? L.C.L.*

If the tripe is inevitable, perhaps the terms you are on are not nearly as good as you would have us believe. And if you feel you must still consort as a couple in public, why did you bother getting divorced in the first place? I believe your friends are acting in good faith — the division of loyalties makes the division of property seem like child's play by comparison.

Do not invite your former husband along to the party. Your friends invited only you, and they must have a good reason for doing so. I would like to think it's because they are courageous enough to refuse to find themselves caught on both sides of the fence. With all this namby-pamby niceness going on about the break-up, the potential for self-torture is enormous. You see Bob and Helen on Tuesday, knowing they had your ex over for dinner on Sunday. You know that they know that he has a new girlfriend, but you're too proud to ask for details and they're too considerate of your feelings to volunteer any. You brag to Bob and Helen about how well you're doing, but come off it: you aren't trying to convince *them*, you're hoping they'll pass the word on to him. It's an absurd little game, and I think your friends are trying to tell you they don't want to play.

Go to the party alone. It might be a chance to meet someone new, but above all it will give you a chance to be yourself. Isn't that one of the principal benefits of breaking up?

WHAT A TANGLED WEB WE WEAVE

It was an evening of exes, currents and putatives. One of the hostess's exes was tending bar, another was there with his current. A woman I know was there with her current, who used to be her ex. My current's ex was there, being openly courted by a putative who was there with his current, no doubt soon to be an ex. There was also a putative of mine who was so miffed at seeing me there with my current that he spent a good part of the evening complaining to all and sundry about my fickleness. Fortunately, we had to leave early to pick up some cats from my ex who was leaving town the following day with his current who is also somebody else's current but that's another story.

Whenever I read a despairing sociological treatise on the anonymity of the big city, I shake my head in amazement. There may be an awful lot of bodies out there, but I think it's human nature to pick out a handful and travel around in circles within the group. Why else is it that, when eavesdropping on other people's conversations in bars (very rude of me, I know, but a professional habit that's deeply ingrained), one is forced to conclude that doctors hang out with other doctors, lawyers with other lawyers, accountants with other accountants — and that they all went to the same school. In our enlightened age, the workplace is by far the meeting ground of choice and, as a result, I know of at least three no-longer-couples who have had to put their heads together to finish a project at the office even as their lawyers were discussing the terms of the divorce.

It's not surprising, therefore, that when we all change lobsters and dance, we are constantly tripping over the skeletons of romances past.

DEAR EVE: *I was dining in one of my favorite restaurants having a* repas intime *(you know, billing and cooing) with my new boyfriend, when I suddenly noticed my former boyfriend wriggling his eyebrows in surprise from a table at the other end of the room. I was frantically searching for a way to introduce the two when my former got up and left without saying good-bye.*

My former and I are (or, perhaps, were) very good friends. My question is this: whose responsibility is it to approach whom first? B.L.

It's not a matter of responsibility, it is a matter of laying one's ego on the line and your former chose not to. He might still be fond of you, but he obviously did not relish the notion of being confronted with proof that life can be lived so well without him. It's not as though he didn't acknowledge your presence (though wriggling one's eyebrows does strike me as a novel form of salutation), so you can't simply accuse him of being rude.

The whole problem of relationships between the one you're with and the one you were with sends me into an absolute tizzy. I was once at a wedding where the best man was a previous lover of the bride, so it obviously can be done. But my ex took to his bed for three days with a migraine when he found out that his current and I were planning to have lunch; afraid we'd compare notes, no doubt.

Don't get me wrong. I have nothing against fostering friendship between the past and present elements of one's life. In fact, if you've spent a long time with someone, who they are is very much a part of who you are, and it's only natural to want to share that aspect of yourself with someone new, along with your favorite books, records and photos from summer camp. But don't rely on a chance encounter at a restaurant when everyone's off guard. Call your ex and ask him if he would like to meet your current and organize an occasion specifically for that purpose. There's no reason why they shouldn't get along — they already have a great deal in common.

DEAR EVE: *My ex and I are still good friends, although we don't see each other often. Should I acknowledge our wedding anniversary in any way? If so, how? It seems kind of heartless to me to pretend the whole thing never happened, but on the other hand, I don't want to start things up again. R.P.*

Why not a bouquet of roses and a bottle of Dom Perignon to celebrate the date your divorce came through? I'm sorry if I tend to sound harsh on the subject, but I honestly don't understand why people split up and then try to pretend they haven't. If you're exes, you're exes and that's all there is to it. I don't assume for a moment that all marriages end acrimoniously; being exes does not preclude being friendly, even loving, with one another.

If that's your situation, by all means send your ex a birthday card or present. Celebrate Christmas or Hanukkah together if that's what you would normally do. In short, treat your ex as you would any other friend — with consideration and generosity. But let the marriage lie.

DIVORCED KIDS

Mommy and Daddy and Baby and Daddy's new girlfriend — the nuclear family for the 1980s. I can't pretend to understand the intricate protocol governing joint custody or any of the new-fangled family situations that are becoming more and more the norm on the social landscape. I've met kids who are literally left on the doorstep on alternate Sunday nights because their parents aren't speaking to each other; I've also met ex-couples who gracefully and gladly ignore past resentments for Thanksgiving or Christmas dinner so their sons and daughters can have a sense of family. The rules are as different in each case as the variations on the family theme which are played out once the original unit of husband and wife has broken into its constituent pieces. Etiquette is based on tradition, and we haven't been at the fragmented family game long enough to have devised a universal code of behavior.

Dear Eve: *I have been dating a very sweet man and, I suppose you could say, his equally charming fourteen-year-old daughter. By that I mean he's divorced and she comes with the territory.*

We all get along really well but, because I haven't known him a very long time, I get a bit nervous when Karen (his daughter) puts on a big show about how nice it is having me around. I don't worry that he's looking for a wife; I do worry that she's looking for a mother.

She has just graduated from junior high and asked me if I would attend the ceremony with her father. "Mommy's going to be there with her new boyfriend," she informed me, "so it's only fair that Daddy bring you." It was all a bit too family for me, so I turned her down. Besides, I had never met Mommy and didn't want to in those circumstances. Now I feel guilty about having hurt her feelings. Was I wrong not to have gone? F.R.

Whoever said the extended family is a thing of the past? If the divorce rate continues on its present skyward course, most children will have two sets of parents and eight sets of grandparents, not to mention ties with who knows how many other adults who are merely passing through. Margaret Mead would have approved.

It's awfully nice to be wanted, but I sympathize with your reservations about being clutched to the family bosom so abruptly. I don't think you were wrong to have declined the invitation: the decision to go public as a couple must be yours and Daddy's, and Daughter mustn't be allowed to pressure you into a commitment you are not as yet ready to make. By the sounds of it, she was also trying to get back at Mommy on Daddy's behalf, which isn't terrifically fair to you.

But to make her feel a bit less rejected, treat her to a small gift or private celebration of her graduation. An outing just the two of you share would be a perfect opportunity to let her know that, although you may not be her family, you'd like to go on being her friend.

Dear Eve: *My boyfriend was previously married and has a six-year-old son who spends weekends with us every fourth week. When we go out, people assume he is ours. Should I explain the situation to them? How do I do it without seeming defensive and without embarrassing my boyfriend or his son? Or me? R.L.*

The way to avoid any misunderstandings is to take the initiative. A six-year-old child qualifies as a person in his own right and should be given his own identity when dealing with others. On your next outing, introduce him to anyone you might meet in a way that leaves no doubt about who's who and what's what. "Mrs. Parker, this is Sean. He's Bill's son and he's visiting us for the weekend." If Mrs. Parker is of the nosy variety, she can pursue the subject at her own peril.

YOU KEEP THE RING, I'LL TAKE THE CAKE

When all is said and done at the end of a relationship, there are still little bits and pieces of it left lying around: a photograph, a borrowed book, a program from a play you once saw together. Some people hang on to every shred for memory's sake; others would just as soon dispose of the evidence. But there are some tokens of love which can't be dispensed with so easily.

DEAR EVE: *The young man I had been seeing for some time gave me his grandmother's ruby ring as a gift. It was not an engagement present since our relationship had not progressed to that stage. Unfortunately, we decided to break up recently. I love the ring, but I realize it also has a great sentimental value for him. Should I give it back? C.B.*

You are very generous to be asking the question in the first place. Since you point out this was not a token of betrothal, the usual protocol (returning the ring if you're calling it quits, keeping it if he is) does not apply. Nor, judging by the sensible tone of your letter, is this a case of rejecting someone by flinging inanimate objects, which were once symbols of affection, back at him.

This particular ring is irreplaceable, though the relationship, unfortunately, proved not to be. By all means return it. Send along a little note saying: "I know how much this gift meant when you gave it. I appreciated it at the time, and I am returning it in the same spirit."

DEAR EVE: *Tradition has tripped me up — literally. When I got married, I observed the English custom of setting aside two tiers of my wedding cake for future use: one was earmarked for the first christening, the second for our twenty-fifth anniversary. Since we weren't planning any children, we indulged in the first one to mark one year of wedded bliss. The wedded bliss didn't go on for much longer, and we are now divorced.*

The other day, while rummaging around in my basement, I stumbled on the tin in which this last vestige of our marriage had been hermetically sealed. It's a perfectly good cake, and I would hate to waste it. Other than sending it to my ex and his new bride to celebrate the christening of their *first child, do you have any ideas for what use I can make of it? J.G.H.*

It's apparently too late to serve it at a divorce party, and bronzing has never appealed to my sense of esthetics, even when it comes to baby shoes. You might take a leaf from your bridesmaid's manual and sleep with it under your pillow until you dream of the man who will be your next husband. But let's face it; hanging on to painful memories is for the birds. I recommend you break the thing up into little pieces and feed it to them on your back porch.

TILL DEATH DO US PART

Dear Eve: *I was involved in a longstanding relationship with a married man which, as far as I know, he managed to keep secret from his wife. I use the past tense because he died recently, and I've been really torn about the best way to pay my last respects. There was an announcement in the paper saying where and when the funeral was to be held. I didn't go, but I wish I had. Do you think it would have been all right for me to attend? E.O.*

Absolutely not. François Truffaut once made a film called *The Man Who Loved Women*, which began and ended with a funeral attended exclusively by women the hero (!) had had affairs with. That sort of thing is all very well and good in the cinema, but it's of dubious taste in real life. His wife doesn't need the shock of an unpleasant revelation on top of her already considerable burden.

I realize that you, like everyone else who has experienced a loss, need to express your grief, but I think you will have to deal with it in private. Visit his grave when the ceremonies are over and done with and leave flowers or some other token of your esteem. Or make a donation in his name to a cause or charity you know he supported. I'm afraid the price of being a mistress is keeping your joys — and sorrows — to yourself.

CHAPTER TEN

Inc. Think

The Corporate Life

Business is as business does. Fads in technological office gadgetry may come and go, but otherwise little seems to change in the corporate world from year to year. Oh sure, IBM junior executives are no longer required to sport United States Marine Corps regulation haircuts and pure-as-the-driven-snow button-down shirts, but it will be at least another millenium before blue jeans are standard garb in the boardrooms of the nation and company policy is determined equally by the president and the night doorman.

The primary rule governing protocol in the business world is respecting the corporate pecking order. The most successful executives are those who have a highly developed sense of hierarchy. Inc. Think today is not that far removed from the mindset of the Ming Court in ancient China. In fact, it must have been easier then because status was color-coded. The Emperor, for example, was the only one permitted to wear yellow. The baubles and bangles on display weren't only for decoration: they signalled the wearer's station in life — a sixteenth-century version, if you will, of keys to the executive washroom.

Although to an untrained observer the business world is remarkably easy-going these days, we haven't really come all that far. You might call your boss Bob instead of Mr. Witherspoon, but that doesn't make him any less your boss. The best-bred company man, despite all the recent stylistic changes, is still the one who knows how to toe the company line.

But, I hear you thinking, what about the growing number of women toting briefcases in to work in the morning? The only difference I see is that now some of the toers are of the female sex.

DISTAFF STAFFERS

It's not that the rules have changed as a result of women in the work force as much as women *don't know the rules* which predate their appearance on the scene. As evidence, I point to the innumerable magazine articles and books (with titles such as *Dress for Success*) which urge women to go into the corporate world disguised as men — three-piece pinstriped suits, albeit with skirts, and all that.

> ***Dear Eve:*** *I am a thirty-five-year-old professional woman who was raised on the etiquette regarding introductions in the fifties, namely that a woman remains seated for anyone who enters the room, except for someone very old or very important, and that a woman shakes hands only if the other person offers a hand first.*
>
> *But now, being in a predominantly male profession, I find I feel more comfortable jumping up with the other men in the room and reaching across the boardroom table to shake hands. I have received a few startled looks from some people and, since I am surrounded by men, I can't look to other women for clues. Have you any guidelines for what today's etiquette demands for this everyday occurrence? J.S.*

The French define ostracism as going through an entire day without having shaken a single hand. In those terms, it seems we're all on the outs with one another, except, for some peculiar reason, in business. I would venture the reason is that the firmness (or limpness) of someone's grasp is considered to be a good indication of what he or she will be like to deal with — a bit of intelligence which doesn't really matter in purely social situations.

Since women have been excluded from business for so long, they have had no reason to practise this particular ritual of nonverbal communication. A languid, ladylike wrist was all that was required to let everyone know one was above the concerns of the more prosaic aspects of life, such as making a living. But since a good, strong handshake literally means business, you are quite right to forget all that lady-of-leisure nonsense and get a good grip on things.

By staying put in your seat until someone deigns to draw attention to your existence, you would, in effect, be saying that you are not really part of the group — that you're not important enough to account for yourself. This might very well set the tone for the rest of the meeting, and I wouldn't be in the least surprised if, somewhere along the line, they expected you to make the coffee. You are right not to let this happen.

The startled looks you have received are from people who don't believe women have any business in business in the first place; by acting the shrinking violet, you would be playing straight to their prejudices. If you're going to do it at all, you may as well do it right. Consider the act of getting up to shake hands simply a gesture of respect toward a superior — or an equal.

Dear Eve: *Our department, until recently, has been all men. We all get along and occasionally go off at lunch together or after work for a beer. We have a new staff member who is a woman, and we all like her enough to want to include her in our sorties. But there was one awkward moment recently when we all went out for a beer. She didn't exactly jump to when it came time to settle. I say we are right to assume she pays her own share, but one of the others thinks we should get it straight with her. What do you say? A.M.*

For once I wish I could say assume away. Theoretically, you're in a much safer position than a man who asks a woman to have dinner with him on a friendly basis and then finds himself stuck with the tab — you *know* she's got a paycheck coming in. It would be ideal if you could do her the honor of treating her like one of the gang in every respect, but she has to prove she thinks of herself as one of the gang first. If she didn't "jump to," she obviously doesn't. Therefore, a small dose of straightness is decidedly in order. Or even, for that matter, a bit of bluntness. "Hey, Louise. Didja get to the bank today? We're all going over to the Ottoman Empire Bar and Grill. If you're solvent, you're welcome to join us."

NO RESERVATIONS ABOUT TRAVEL

DEAR EVE: *I attend a business conference once a year and make valuable contacts during official sessions and more informal, after-hours gatherings. I know this is somewhat unusual, because most of the women on these trips still order room-service and avoid the spur-of-the-moment (but very productive) sessions, in the misguided interests of propriety. I have never had any doubts that my actions might be misinterpreted because I know how to say "yes" to the dinner-and-drinks invitations which might prove useful and "no" to the post-midnight knocks on my door.*

I pride myself on going where no woman has gone before, and it has really paid off in terms of increased sales as well as awareness of what is going on in my industry. So I was absolutely stunned when, after my last trip, my boss called me into his office and gave me a dressing-down for "unladylike behavior." It seems that one of my male co-workers had brought my presence in the hotel bar to his attention. Is there any firm but polite way to inform my boss that I intend to go on as I always have in the company's interest, or do I have to lock myself away in my room next year? P.L.

The snitches of the schoolyard are ever with us. Perhaps your colleague feels threatened by your success, but even without resorting to ten-cent psychoanalysis, it's obvious he does not count you as a member of the fraternity of junketeers. He has violated one of the primary rules of its code of conduct: whatever happens on a junket after-hours is strictly off the record. Since business trips are legendary for their excesses, I'm sure you could have countered by informing your boss that your co-worker and the bartender were on a first-name basis by closing time, or that the sight of him being deposited unceremoniously in front of his hotel room door did not do credit to the company name. But *that* would be unladylike.

Before trying to win your point with your boss, you should make peace in the ranks or the whole problem may just repeat itself. Explain to your co-worker that you, like him, are only trying to do your job. He might not approve of women in the work force, much less on business trips, but his convictions are out of date. You are in your present position because someone thought you capable of the job, and his efforts to undermine your effectiveness won't set the clock back to the days when women "knew their place" — which was decidedly not at Harry's Hideaway with an order book in one hand and a dry martini in the other.

As for your boss, tell him with a smile that you realize the company is not underwriting your expenses in Tucson or wherever for the purpose of allowing you to catch up on reruns of "Hollywood Squares." You are doing business as business has always been done, and he has only to check your sales record to know that you are good at it.

MARRIAGE ON COMPANY TIME

In the bad old days, companies bought two bodies for the price of one. Unmarried men were rarely considered for important positions, and any candidate for a private parking space had to parade his missus around to prove that she would not be a discredit to the corporate image. Women, you'll remember, once married not only men but their jobs as well (as in Pam married a lawyer, not Pam married Dave). There was no greater glory for them than passing muster on the night The Boss Came to Dinner. My mother's "career" consisted of following my father around the globe and earning her keep as an ever-gracious hostess to local bigwigs. She did it extraordinarily well, but I don't know that she ever got a promotion.

Those days are coming to an end as more and more women have arrived at the conclusion that it's much more rewarding to actually sign the contracts than to arrange the celebratory dinner.

DEAR EVE: *My wife recently got a terrific job with a very large company. It is taking up a lot of her time, but the financial and emotional rewards are obviously worth it. I'm doing my bit by taking on additional duties around the house to lend support to the cause, but, unfortunately, she doesn't think it's enough. The place where she works is an incredibly social shop — it seems every other week there is some sort of social function. At Christmas there was the usual round of parties, then in January there were two dinner dances in honor of retiring vice-presidents. This month there has already been a cocktail party to welcome a visiting muckety-muck from head office, and they're planning a fund-raising affair for charity in March.*

My wife expects me to squire her to all these events. There is no question of her not going, and she insists my presence scores her additional Brownie points with her boss, who is a gung-ho family type. Besides, she argues, wives have always been expected to do it for husbands. I'm not terribly outgoing even with people I've known for a long time, and all this partying is taking its toll on my nerves. How can I convince her to let me stay home with my pipe and slippers? H.F.S.

Your wife's company is apparently enlightened enough to hire a woman for an important position but old guard enough to want to carry on "the corporation is just one big happy family" routine.

Inform your wife that even the staid old diplomatic corps is loosening up a bit; for instance, I am well aware of the stand of Jeane Kirkpatrick, American ambassador to the United Nations, on Argentina, but I can't honestly say that I remember the last time I saw her husband's name on a White House guest list.

You presumably have a job and friends of your own, so you don't need to rely on your wife for your social life the way company spouses used to. Tell her if she's liberated enough to make her way in the working world, she's liberated enough to eat rubber chicken on her own. Sharing domestic chores and providing a sympathetic ear after a hard day at the office go without saying; making chit-chat with the fellows in accounting is above and beyond the call of a liberated husband's duty. If you do not wish to spend your nights traipsing behind your wife as she makes the round of corporate shindigs, you're within your rights to sit out a few.

DEAR EVE: *My husband and I are planning to spend a few days in New York to attend a family wedding. Since my company's headquarters are there, I phoned my counterpart (whom I have never met) to suggest a brief courtesy visit. She seemed to be delighted and immediately invited me to lunch. We don't have any particular business with each other, other than getting acquainted, so I suppose, technically, it will be more of a social occasion than a professional one. My husband doesn't particularly care to be left alone in a strange place and enjoys meeting new people. Would it be okay to bring him along for lunch? S.M.*

It's fine by me, if it's fine by the person picking up the tab. Your colleague will probably justify the lunch as a business expense, and I'm sure the company's largesse can stretch to accommodate one more helping of quiche and spinach salad. The etiquette of such a situation is simply to clear the way beforehand.

Since you apparently didn't advise her of this particular wrinkle when you spoke to her, call her again a couple of days before you are scheduled to meet on the pretense of confirming your appointment. Give her the option of saying no, but I doubt very much that she will. After you have gone over the details of time and place, tell her, "I forgot to mention that my husband Jerry will be with me on the trip. He'd very much like to meet you, too. Would it be a problem if he joined us?" The only way it would be a problem is if she's made reservations at a restaurant which requires anyone not related to the maitre d' to wait three months for the first available table. By giving her plenty of time to adjust to a different game plan, you give her a chance to change the venue if necessary.

With all the talk of showing your hostess some consideration, let's not forget your husband. You and your colleague will want to fill each other in on the doings at your respective offices and will find yourselves discussing business despite your stated intentions to the contrary. Keep it to a minimum or he'll suddenly remember how much he enjoys solitary visits to art galleries. Make him a part of the proceedings or all of you will start to wonder why you went to the trouble of making it a threesome to begin with.

BUSINESSMAN'S SPECIAL

The business lunch is one of the most civilized benefits of working. Not only can it be written off on an expense account, or on income tax returns if you're self-employed, but it can also provide a relaxed atmosphere in which to handle business affairs. (I said *business* affairs; trysting is another matter altogether and is not, as far as I know, a deductible expense.) There's something about meeting over a ham and asparagus omelet that makes people involved feel better disposed to reaching an agreement than if they are separated by the expanse of a mahogany desk. But it is only apparently more relaxed; there are as many rules governing noon get-togethers as there are at any other time of the day. (See also "Unwritten Rules of the Business Lunch," page 159.)

DEAR EVE: *I very often have business meetings with my clients over lunch. If you are meeting an associate at a restaurant, whose name should the reservation be under? Does it matter if he has a more senior position with his company than I have with mine? F.F.*

The person who proposes, disposes. If you are issuing the invitation, no matter what your rank, you set the terms, time and place. You (or your secretary, if you are high enough in the corporate stratosphere to have one) should call the restaurant to make all the necessary arrangements. Be forewarned that the maitre d' will then know who to stick for the bill, and, unless your associate is willing to arm-wrestle you for the privilege, you also get to pick up the tab.

DEAR EVE: *I am a business woman who often takes her clients out for lunch. I've learned to handle men who insist they should be paying by beating them to the bill when it comes, and informing them that it all goes on my expense account when they protest. My problem is not with them, it is with waiters.*

I usually pay with a credit card so that I'll have a record of the meeting. Invariably, when the waiter brings the credit card slip back to the table to be signed, he puts it in front of my male guest, and I have to reach across for it under his disapproving gaze. It may seem trivial, but it's one more bit of embarrassment I don't need when I'm trying to put a man at ease about my paying in the first place. How do you recommend I handle it? S.W.

I think many waiters are catching on, although you obviously have not been as lucky as I have in this regard. In a similar situation not so long ago, one bright fellow placed the chit right smack dab in the middle of the table with a flourish and flashed both my guest and me a grin to let us know that the rightful owner could claim it. I tipped him generously for his tact.

Why waiters can't read the name on the card, I'll never know, but they don't, it's true. I suggest that instead of simply placing the credit card on the bill plate and leaving it for the waiter to pick up whenever he has a moment, you call him over and hand it to him with a smile. Unless he's got a powerfully short memory, he should know to whom it is to be returned.

THE COMPANY WE KEEP

The appalling truth is that we spend a greater part of our lives with the folks at the office than with our husbands or wives. We choose the latter, but have little say in the choice of the former — unless, that is, we marry one of our co-workers and then there's no safe place.

It's rare that one can tell someone to bugger off unless one owns the store. But if your boss is the bane of your life, the Lord save us all. Being a marketing genius may get you far in your field, but not as far as knowing how to neutralize the offensiveness of the fellow down the hall short of putting in for a transfer.

DEAR EVE: *I work in one of those open plan offices without sound baffles, which is rather nice because I usually feel I'm part of everything that's going on. But I have a co-worker who has a particularly loud voice. When he speaks on the phone, the decibel level suggests he's talking to Dar es Salaam, not downtown. I suspect he doesn't even need a phone — all he has to do is open the window to converse. Alas, there are no windows here that open.*

I'm faced with the unpleasant prospect of tearing off my sock and stuffing it in his mouth. Is there a polite way of getting myself out of his business activities? J.K.

Calling a person's attention to an annoying trait is never very polite, no matter what television commercials for mouthwash might have led you to believe. But rudeness is occasionally necessary to preserve one's sanity, and one could argue that the ends justify the meanness. Forcing someone to savor the taste of an odiferous polyester and wool blend argyle is a bit extreme, however.

Your colleague doesn't strike me as the subtle type, but subtlety is always the preferable first approach. When he has hung up after his next harangue, you might say, in a sympathetic tone, "Boy, this office sure is noisy. I find it really hard to carry on a phone conversation, too. I can barely make out what the other person is saying, and I find myself yelling over the typewriter clatter. Maybe we should ask Mr. Boss if we could set up a quiet corner just for the phones."

If you think that's letting him off the hook too lightly, point out to him that a lot of progress has been made in communications technology since the phone was invented. Alexander Graham Bell might have had to yell to get Mr. Watson's attention but these days, why even Dar es Salaam comes in clear as a (uh-oh ... there's no stopping it now) bell.

Then there's always the blackmail route as a last resort. When he's off the phone, parrot the conversation he's just had back to him in the guise of an interest in his affairs. "So, you were talking to your accountant. I think the idea of getting the company to lease a car for you instead of giving you a raise is a great idea for saving on income tax." It might get him paranoid enough to seek some privacy for himself — and, in the process, grant you yours.

DEAR EVE: *I have a pet peeve that I am sure is shared by many people north of the Mason-Dixon Line. While the winter season is upon us, so are colds, flu and other ailments that nature strews in the path of our lungs and upper respiratory tracts. However, there are those who, no matter how severe their ailment, insist on hauling their posteriors into the office, theater, restaurant and, yea, even unto my dinner parties. By so doing, all those who come into contact with them run a somewhat greater risk of infection than a philandering sailor. To compound the problem, in the office they insist on explaining to all who notice their ailment that they are there at great personal sacrifice. This is, to my mind, inconsiderate in the extreme.*

Could you advise your readers that behavior such as this is usually unappreciated, both physiologically and psychologically, by those upon whom the above deeds are perpetrated? V.C.

I can sympathize with your desire to stay healthy, but I think putting the rest of the world in quarantine will not guarantee it. Some people's definition of consideration, apparently, includes getting their work done and honoring social commitments. I can comply with your request to the extent of reminding people that bed rest, vitamin C and chicken soup are the best medicine. But I have to refer to a Higher Authority when it comes to eliminating all sniffles and sneezes from public places.

DEAR EVE: *Please tell me how a professional woman should handle things when a man decides to put his shoes (with feet in them, of course) on top of his desk. Being left to maintain eye contact over a ten-inch sole is very uncomfortable. C.D.*

You realize, of course, that what he's signalling is the fact he's in charge. You could choose to remain standing during your next interview, thus giving yourself some advantage of vantage point. But if your want to get a message across to him (over his feet), I suggest the next time you walk into his office, you equip yourself with a phone book. Tell him, with a smile on your face and in a friendly manner, that you need it to sit on when your view is obscured by his lower extremities.

DEAR EVE: *One of my co-workers is seeing a shrink. I won't comment on her need for one, but she is driving all of us crazy. You can't ask her if she has the report on Tuesday's meeting handy without getting an earful on how she is finally overcoming her fear of authority by dealing with the negative emotions resulting from a critical comment made by her father when she was six. It's always "My shrink says this" or "My shrink says that." The days she actually has an appointment with her doctor are the worst because we are then treated to a full progress report if one of us says so much as "Hi, how are you?" Is there any way to get her to keep her therapy to herself? D.Y.*

The Catholic Church was really on to something when it made confession a sacrament. The problem with angst is that it tends to go on and on, unlike a gall bladder operation which is usually a one-shot deal and can be dispensed with in a mere three dinner parties. Your colleague isn't being rude — she's being a bloody bore and, to date, no cure has been found for this appalling social affliction. No point in telling her this because — heaven forfend! — your "hostility" will set the course of her analysis back by at least ten years and your comments will provide dissection fodder for another round of visits.

A little psychology is called for here. Try to draw her into a discussion of the principles of doctor-patient confidentiality. How would she feel if her psychiatrist was referring to her as "an interesting case of paranoid anxiety neurosis" on the squash court? Let her draw her own conclusions.

DEAR EVE: *What are you supposed to do when you're in someone's office and she gets an important or personal phone call? Should you leave? F.D.*

Aha. Your basic captive audience scenario. Most uncomfortable, I quite agree. Apparently you were not in your colleague's office to discuss a matter of life and death or she would have asked her secretary to hold all calls. So, when one does come in and your colleague doesn't inform the caller that she is in a meeting and will call him back later, you have two options. You can either signal your intention to leave and return when she's through or you can commit the sales graph on the wall to memory. Both are correct when you have no indication from her which she would prefer. If you stay, act uninterested for the duration and, when she finally rests the receiver in its cradle, don't try to get into her good graces by saying, "So, you and your husband aren't getting on too well these days." It is up to her to indicate she wishes to share more than she already has with you. If she mutters, "Now, where were we?" that means you've heard absolutely nothing.

THE PERKS

***DEAR EVE:** I work for a large company which provides business cards for its senior employees. My boss has asked me several times if I want some made up, but I've always said no because, frankly, I don't know what you do with business cards. Do people still use them? I sometimes receive letters with a business card stapled to them instead of a letterhead or a return address typed on, but I don't like it. Tell me, am I wrong in not availing myself of my boss's offer? P.I.*

I can see it now — legions of unemployed butlers crying in their beer over this one. You're right: a card on a silver salver to announce the presence of a gentleman caller is definitely passé. But you're wrong in believing business cards have no use at all. They may no longer serve as a way of saying hello, but they're just the ticket for saying good-bye.

Suppose you're meeting an important client for the first time at a restaurant. You agree in principle, but you need a few more particulars from him before you can clinch the deal. So, rather than fumbling around for a pen and a piece of paper in your briefcase (or trying to beg, borrow or steal same from the waiter), you reach gracefully into your wallet, fish out a little white rectangle, hand it over and say, "Here's where you can send the material."

It's so terribly elegant. Your business associate will be grateful not only for having been spared the sight of your grovelling about endlessly to carry out a relatively simple procedure, but also because, right there in black and white (or brown and beige, if your company is frightfully chic) is all the information he needs: the correct spelling of your name, your title and the precise location of your cubbyhole.

Or say you decide on the spur of the moment to drop in on a client you have never met. She's not in her office, and the receptionist doesn't feel like taking a message from someone who might prove to be the Fuller Brush Man. So, rather than insist fruitlessly, you take out your calling card, flip it over and write on the back: "Sorry I missed you. I realize I should have made an appointment, but I was in the neighborhood. Please give me a call to arrange a meeting at your convenience." The name, rank and telephone number will speak for themselves.

Evidence of the usefulness of business cards can be found in the variety of accessories to accommodate them available at stationery stores. I staple them into my address book rather than bothering to decipher phone numbers and street names. I don't like them as a replacement for letterhead, but material sent through the mail with a card on which is written "With my compliments" makes me feel it matters to someone that I read what's enclosed. And I have no objections whatsoever to being sent a bouquet of roses for my desk from someone who is pleased with my work or wishes to apologize for the dreadful scene at the end of the convention. Tell your boss you've changed your mind.

CHRISTMAS BONUS

DEAR EVE: *I work in an office where I have a boss in the strict sense of the word and also answer to four other people in the department. I'm wondering: should I give them all Christmas presents? This is my first year at this job but where I worked before it was customary to give the boss something. Also, could you suggest something appropriate and inexpensive? B.W.*

It pays to take the Boy Scout motto seriously. Every office has its own protocol when it comes to presents, and I don't think you should go all out without doing some checking first. Don't wait till the last moment and second-guess the situation; you might embarrass people with uncalled for generosity. Ask around as far ahead of time as possible so that people don't make the connection and will therefore respond disinterestedly.

Office presents should never be intimate. A bottle of some sort is always nice (unless your boss is notorious for his drinking habits). And monogrammed pens, a coffee mug or plants are always appreciated. (See also "Christmas Without Tears," page 161.)

OVERHEARD AT THE WATER COOLER

Where would we be without rumors? Without them, we wouldn't know that Russia had invaded Afghanistan. (What is the six o'clock news anyway but an institutionalized version of gossip mongering?) We wouldn't know that John Wayne's real first name was Marion, that the house down the street went for $123,000 and that there is a position open in product testing. But most of all, we would have nothing to say to one another over lunch, and life would be ferociously boring. Pass the gossip mill, please.

DEAR EVE: *I work at an office where news travels at an alarming rate. My problem is that one of my male co-workers, who has always been very kind to me, recently suggested I accompany him on his winter vacation. I assumed he was joking and went along with him, saying it was a wonderful idea. Unfortunately, he doesn't seem to be taking as light-hearted a view of the matter as I have been, and now I'm afraid he actually expects me to go along with him. How can I explain the trip is out of the question without hurting his feelings? E.D.*

Ask your friend out to lunch, away from the prying eyes and ears of Peyton Place Inc. Bring along a beautifully wrapped going away present — a pair of down slippers if he's going someplace cold, a gaily colored beach towel if he's headed for sunnier climes. Explain to him that the gift will have to take your place on the trip.

DEAR EVE: *I recently took out a woman who works with me in a large insurance office. Normally I steer clear of in-office romances, and I explained my feelings on the matter to her before we went out. We agreed not to let anyone know we were seeing each other. A week later, however, during a coffee break, a few things were said which convinced me that everybody in the building knows about our date. One thing's for sure: I'll never date her again. What can I do to stop her blabbing more? A.T.*

I'm sure it was Oscar Wilde (it usually is) who said, "The only thing worse than people talking about you is people not talking about you." If you made enough of an impression on the lady for her to wish to spread the word, you should be flattered. She was obviously discreet enough not to enumerate any embarrassing details or the kaffeeklatsch chatter would not have taken place while you were within earshot.

As for your concern that she will discuss the liaison in the future, you have already solved your problem. If you never take her out again, there will be nothing more to say.

CHAPTER ELEVEN

Public Places

Public places are first and foremost public. Lest you shrug that off merely as a statement of the obvious, let me remind you that manners have always been defined as the small considerations which facilitate human contact. And nowhere are they more severely tested than in the no man's land of subways, sidewalks, theaters, shopping malls, restaurants and any form of travel. I refer to them all as no man's land because there's no host to disapprove, and the risk of not being invited back doesn't hang over your head to keep you from misbehaving.

It's a cinch to sit in someone's living room, cross your legs, say "please" and "thank you" and go through all the other motions of politesse when you're psychologically prepared for having to put on a show. Your true civility is tried when you have to navigate your way through a crowd, wait in a check-in line at the airport or get to the end of a restaurant meal in such a way that the other diners don't wish they had stayed home and finished last night's meatloaf. I don't presume to have the answer to the rising crime rate, but you must admit fewer tempers would be riled if people didn't shove themselves through crowded doorways, stand to any side they please on escalators and carry on conversations with their neighbors throughout the showing of a movie. If I bump into someone who's in a dreadful hurry, I always mutter "Excuse me," even if to his fleeing shadow. It's a reflex and I've found myself feeling quite silly apologizing to thin air, but it's like so many other things in life — practice makes perfect.

The fact that someone is a stranger is more, not less, reason to be on your best behavior. Sneer all you will at the great unwashed, you are one of them, as far as I'm concerned, if you are guilty of any of the following: parading up and down the street with your radio at full blast; not offering your seat on the bus to an elderly or overburdened passenger, regardless of sex; snarling at supermarket cashiers; stubbing a cigarette out on a plate of unfinished food anywhere, public or private; butting into any line whatsoever; or ordering waiters around as though you were the Czar of Russia and still haven't realized that the Revolution has left you unemployed. Besides, you never know who you might run into.

A friend of the family, a French count as it happens, was driving home late one night, his mind no doubt on the myriad pleasures afforded by the City of Light, when he rear-ended another car. Its driver, an extremely well-dressed woman of "a certain age" leapt out and launched into a string of epithets primarily to do with his dubious parentage, to which the French language is so eminently suited. When she had finished her tirade, the count shook his head. "Mother," he said. "I'm surprised at you."

ON THE MENU

DEAR EVE: *I was with a large group in a restaurant — a restaurant that advertises itself as a homey sort of place, with uncovered wooden tables and long benches. There weren't too many other people there, and one of us happened to have a guitar with him, so he started to play. If anybody minded, they certainly didn't say so.*

After a nice, long, leisurely meal, we settled the bill, left a tip and got up to leave, only to have the restaurant owner descend upon us with all guns blazing. He proceeded to preach at us about abusing his premises. He said we were guests at his establishment and had no right to behave as we did. I think it was a straight exchange of goods — we paid for the food and the use of the premises — and his "guest" argument doesn't wash. Am I right? K.H.

Yes and no. He was certainly wrong to have acted as he did. Instead, he should have asked you not to make yourselves quite as at home when you first began your musical interlude, or he should have interceded on behalf of the other diners had they objected to the impromptu concert. But to take you to task so long after the fact — and to end your evening on such a down note — was not very fair. Had he reprimanded you earlier, you would havc had a chancc to show your displcasurc with his attitudc by at least not leaving a tip. Now the only way to let him know you're mad is never to patronize his beanery again.

But his argument about your being his "guests" is not all that far off the mark. A restaurant or hotel provides atmosphere as well as food or lodging. Owners go to considerable pains to decorate their premises, offer entertainment and tailor their bills of fare to attract a specific sort of clientele. So, you see, there's considerably more involved than a straight exchange of goods, as you put it — unless you feel ambience is a "good" which can simply be purchased. ("I'll take a pound and a half of pleasant vibes, please. Don't bother to wrap it.")

It is very much the owner's business (and his right) to set down some guidelines for the behavior he expects of those who avail themselves of what he has to offer. For instance, clubs may demand that members wear only whites on the tennis courts, and night spots that all their visitors be Beautiful People. I know of one owner of a roast beef establishment who refused admittance to a group of Boy Scouts (*Boy Scouts*, for heaven's sake) because he did not feel that their uniforms conformed to his jacket-and-tie rule. More than one bar in the annals of inn-keeping has asked rowdies to take their trade elsewhere. To avoid any repetition of the unpleasant scene you've described, may I suggest you order in Chinese food for your next *soirée musicale*?

Dear Eve: *What is the correct way to signal a waiter? P.W.*

The way you would any other human being. Say "excuse me" if he's within earshot, or wave your hand discreetly in his direction if he's across the room. If he's not visible, ask any passing staff member if he or she could request his presence at your table.

Snapping your fingers and yelling "Garçon!" should only be used by actors in revivals of Feydeau farces.

Dear Eve: *We went out for an after-theater dinner to a posh restaurant which turned out to be a disaster — too* *loud, too crowded, slow service and bad food. But the killer was the conversation of the people at the next table: four plastered, polyester-clad businessmen who persisted in discussing, loudly and grossly, the physical attributes of women they know. I'm no prude, but it really put me off. There was nowhere else to sit, and we were too hungry at that hour to go elsewhere. Would it have been legit to request them to change the topic of conversation? W.J.*

Waiter, please send four snifters of hemlock to that table with our compliments. I'm afraid, even though I do it for a living, it is extremely bad form to tell strangers how to behave. You could have asked the maitre d' to request a lowering of the volume on your behalf. As for the contents of the broadcast, however, you are not entitled to play censor — it's bad enough that governments do it.

If you left before they did, a parting shot in their direction, while definitely not good manners, might have at least satisfied your frustration. You could have smiled sweetly as you put on your coat and said, "Thank you for settling a dispute my friend and I were having. He maintains there aren't any Neanderthals still living, but you have just won my point for me."

DEAR EVE: *My husband and I have gone out for dinner with a foursome to two ethnic restaurants. On both occasions, the other men seemed to take great delight in loudly imitating the stereotypical characteristics of the ethnic group whose food we were eating (not deliberately insulting, I would say, just high spirits). My husband and I found this terribly embarrassing, especially since we had visited these two places several times and were beginning to think of ourselves as regulars. What does one do in a situation like this, bearing in mind that we'd like to keep our friends as well as our local eateries on our side? G.F.*

You can dress 'em up, but you can't take 'em out. While rapping total strangers on the knuckles is a no-no, assuming responsibility for a group so that others won't feel inclined to rap *you* on the knuckles is laudable. The kind of comments you describe, although not "deliberately" insulting, can be hurtful, and you and your husband were quite right to be indignant on behalf of the people at whom they were aimed.

I don't know why you want to keep these friends if that's the kind of louts they are. Far better to be able to show your face again in a restaurant you enjoy than to worry about insulting people whose skins appear to be made of Naugahyde. Tell them in no uncertain terms that you do not wish to be associated with such displays of insensitivity. Show them that you mean it by moving to another table if necessary.

Dear Eve: *Some friends of mine were in from out of town, and we decided to make a festive occasion of it by going to a very posh restaurant. They were meeting my new boyfriend for the first time, and, needless to say, I wanted everyone to get along. All went well until we got to dessert. One of the visitors couldn't finish hers, so my boyfriend did. He often does this at home, but it seemed out of place in public, among strangers. Was he rude? L.W.*

Yes, but I'm on his side. This is not a case of all the poor starving children in India — more likely, all the poor starving busboys in the kitchen — but why should perfectly good *marrons glacés* (at seven dollars a serving) be allowed to go to waste? I feel the most civilized contribution of Chinese restaurants to our society is the institution of doggie bags. Human ones are fine by me, as long as they ask first and don't reach across the table to pick up the goodies with their fingers.

PATIENCE IS NOT A VIRTUE

Dear Eve: *What can you do if you're waiting to be served at a department store counter and somebody who has come along after you gets the sales clerk's attention before you do? G.L.*

Clear your throat loudly. Say, "Excuse me. I was here first." Smile consolingly at the offender and tell the sales clerk what it is you want. Standing up for yourself is not rude. People who fear that it is spend an inordinate amount of time hanging around counters, only to discover that what they're looking for is out of stock.

ON SHOW

Everyone I know is decidedly opposed to movie censorship. Well, I'm for it. I don't think anyone should be allowed to tamper with what's shown on the screen, but I think certain members of the movie-going public should be severely cut down to size. I propose we establish a

Board of Movie Manners (and I, ahem, humbly offer my services as chairman) which would deal with all the late-arrivers, chronic seat-changers, popcorn-chewers, unwrappers of candy and narrators of plot. I want them deemed unfit for human consumption and legislated out of existence. Let them stay at home in front of the TV set where they belong.

The kind of unthinking crassness practised in most downtown theaters occasionally forces one to resort to ill-bred tactics. I've tried "hush" and "ssssshhh" to no avail so many times that I find nothing short of a heartfelt "Shut up, you morons!" seems to work. When the offenders, as is so often the case, are husky teenage boys, I consider myself lucky to escape with nothing more serious than a vicious retaliatory tongue-lashing. I therefore bow to my superior: a man, seeing a thriller for the second time, who was so annoyed by the incessant chatter of three women behind him that he rose ten minutes into the film, turned to his tormentors and explained in minute detail whodunit and why, then stormed magnificently out of the auditorium.

Not all rudeness is the exclusive precinct of the local Bijou, but movies are a more democratic art form than opera, ballet or the symphony. I don't wish to sound too elitist, but there's something about paying thirty-five dollars a ticket that inspires people to be more respectful of the show.

There are certain aspects of etiquette that follow their own muse (such as the letter about concerts which follows), but for the most part, the primary thing to keep in mind is: You Are Not Alone. As one no-nonsense curmudgeon put it: "If you want to eat, go to McDonald's; if you want to talk, throw a party; if you want to hoot and holler, go to a football game; and if you want to make love, then go to bed."

DEAR EVE: *My husband and I have subscription tickets to a concert series. Since we sent away for them rather late, they are far from being the best seats in the house. At every concert we have attended thus far, there have been better seats which remained empty. Several times we have sneaked down into them when it was apparent their occupants weren't going to turn up. Yet I can't help feeling guilty about it and wondering if it's okay to do so. It hasn't happened yet, but what should we say and do if someone arrives to claim the seats after the concert has begun? S.B.*

It is ruder to arrive late and interrupt an audience's enjoyment of a performance than it is to make use of facilities which would otherwise go to waste. Seats are not owned; they are rented (unless some culture-minded philanthropist has added a proviso to his will which calls for the hall to be demolished if the practice of reserving front row center for his ghost is not upheld). I once had the misfortune to be seated behind a pillar, which did nothing to enhance my enjoyment of the ballet I had hocked my grandfather's gold watch to see. My enjoyment was even less enhanced by the presence of two gentlemen (and I use the term loosely) seated to my left who loathed the principal dancers and did not hesitate to say so for the benefit of all within hearing range. When, to my enormous relief, one of them did not return to claim his seat for the second act, I slid over only to be given a thorough lecture on the sanctity of private property. "What do you think you're doing!" he bellowed. "That's my seat. I paid for it and you can't sit in it!" I had no choice but to retreat to my pillar where I managed to enjoy the left half of the remaining two acts. When the last bow had been taken and my neighbor at one remove was about to leave, I couldn't resist a parting shot. "Excuse me, sir," I said with a great show of concern, "You're forgetting your seat. Aren't you going to take it home with you, seeing as you've paid for it?"

I don't recommend fistfights at cultural events — they detract from the artists' share of the spotlight. Should the rightful occupants of the seats you've usurped arrive to claim them, first and foremost, avoid a fuss. Simply say, "Excuse us," and return as unobtrusively as possible to your proper places, if no one else is sitting in them.

DEAR EVE: *If a movie theater is crowded and a very tall person sits down in front of you, is it all right to tap him on the shoulder and ask him to scrunch down? M.A.*

I don't see why not, as long as you do it tactfully and remember to say please. Tall people, like other visible minorities, tend to be quite aware of what sets them apart and try to minimize those differences. In other words, they will usually "scrunch down," as you put it, of their own accord. If you are unfortunate enough to be stuck behind one who insists on bearing his six-foot eight-inch frame regally, a gentle request for consideration is not out of place. But wait until the credits are rolling (not after twenty minutes, and needless to say, do it quietly) unless you know well ahead of time that the film is subtitled. I recommend this delay because while the house lights are on, one is apt to forget the screen is usually placed above eye-level and the audience will be looking up, not straight ahead. If the person's head is indeed blocking your view, anything other than "Hey buddy, you think I can see through you?" will do.

DEAR EVE: *Why do people insist on ignoring "No Smoking" signs? The last time I was at the movies, two kids next to me puffed away non-stop. It's not that I am one of those militant anti-smokers; on the contrary, I am a smoker myself and I get really frustrated trying to keep rules while others break them. Should this happen again, what should I say or do? P.L.*

It is not only impolite to smoke in non-smoking sections, it is also against the law in some places. Inform the miscreants of this fact and, if that fails to produce results, find an usher. He is likely to be a kid working for a bit of extra money after school and is so awed by the authority a uniform provides that he will welcome an opportunity to exert it. Sic 'im at 'em.

THE STARS ARE OUT TONIGHT

DEAR EVE: *On a number of occasions I have spotted very famous showbiz personalities on the street or in restaurants and nightclubs. I am not a groupie or an autograph hound and, frankly, think little of the work of many of these people, so I generally leave them alone. But every so often I do see someone whose work I have greatly admired over the years and feel I would like to make human contact to thank them and tell them how I feel. Is this wrong? When people tell me they like what I do, I feel very flattered. Is there an acceptable way to approach someone famous on a street or in a restaurant without appearing too tacky? Y.W.S.*

I have the opposite problem: how to get *rid* of someone famous — Donald Sutherland. I swear, he follows me everywhere I go. I've run into him at the airport, in restaurants and once in broad daylight we shared a sidewalk on one of the city's busiest streets. He has even tracked me all the way to Montreal. I just can't seem to shake him. Mr. Sutherland, if you are reading this, please leave me alone.

You are not wrong in assuming that most people whose work

is public enjoy being acknowledged. If they didn't, what would be the point in becoming famous? (Please note, however, that whatever I say in this regard does not apply to Greta Garbo.)

The first rule of Stalking the Wild Celebrity is to avoid using "Aren't you ...?" as an opening line. If you aren't sure that this is the party to whom you wish to be speaking, you have no business starting up a conversation in the first place. Stars are a cagey lot; Faye Dunaway, I understand, always answers that question with, "No, but I've been told I look a lot like her." So there goes your chance to invite her home for tea.

Choose your moment carefully. Finding yourself in the ladies' room cubicle adjacent to Margaret Trudeau's is not the right place to inquire if she and Pierre have ever tried marriage counseling. If you spot your quarry in a restaurant, let him at least get the business of eating over with before you attack. Otherwise, you run the risk of forcing him to be doubly rude: not inviting you to join him and talking with his mouth full.

In general, once you have approached the idol in question, act as you would with anyone to whom you have not been introduced. Introduce yourself and state your business. Unless you're Vincent Canby, your business shouldn't be to tell him his last film was awful. You may ask for an autograph, if you're so inclined, but what use someone's signature on a scrap of paper is if you're not planning to forge cheques I'll never understand.

Don't dally unless asked to, for your own sake as well as the star's. If you hang around long enough, you might discover the sad truth that celebrities are really very ordinary (and sometimes quite boring) people with an aura of glitz around them which is often not even of their own making.

ON THE ROAD

When travelling, some people, it seems, check their manners along with their luggage. It's as though the doorway to the airport or train station marks a boundary beyond which the disapprobation of Mother, the neighbors and the boss's uptight secretary cannot reach. For too many, the delicious anonymity of being in transit means there are no rules any more.

Why else would impeccably dressed matrons, the sort who would rather die than forget to send a thank-you letter, shove their way to the head of the ticket line without so much as a by-your-leave? Why else would middle-aged men, whose exquisitely tailored suits suggest they are company presidents, stuff fourteen minature bottles of Rémy into their attachés because they believe the offer of unlimited free booze should be taken literally? Why else would young mothers, who of all people should know what it means to be harried, allow their five-year-olds to run around the train station screaming out the words to the Sesame Street theme song, or run flight attendants ragged because they didn't think to pack enough diapers for their babe in arms?

It makes no difference if they're flying first class, or travelling by chartered bus or on a train, off to visit Aunt Gertrude in Nova Scotia, zipping to Tokyo on business or junketing to Las Vegas. This grand, egalitarian age of travel has come to mean that everyone has a right to be an utter boor, no matter how much (or how little) he has paid for his seat.

You expect me, no doubt, to wax lyrical about the Good Old Days when only the rich could afford to see the world, when passengers stepped out of their limousines at the airport or dockside decked out in their finest duds, and when washrooms at the train station said "Ladies" and "Gentlemen" and meant it. Well, I wouldn't trade all the nostalgia in the world for the ability to take off to Vancouver in my blue jeans without having to take out a second mortgage. No, no, my dears — it's not that travel isn't what it used to be, it's that manners aren't what they used to be.

The chaos! The chaos! It makes you wonder why anyone would ever want to go anywhere. My nomination for The Most Dreaded Moment at airports is when boarding is announced. Airlines have tried to cut down the confusion by boarding passengers with special needs (invalids, parents with small children) first and then letting everyone else on, back to front. But it's still bedlam. "Someone's been told there's a prize for getting on first," one exasperated flight attendant once muttered to me. "They just won't believe their seat will still be there by the time they reach it."

When on the move, neatness counts all right — but not when there are 483 people still left waiting to get on board. While you're folding your coat, stashing your gear and getting your favorite reading material out of your overnight bag, there are all the rest of us behind you, waiting patiently to get by you on the way to seats 21 A, B, C, D, and E. *Settle down, class, please*. Most of it can wait till we're rolling.

DEAR EVE: *I travel alone a great deal, which means I often wind up on planes and trains seated next to* *people who want to know the story of my life. Most people take the hint when I'm not feeling talkative (I always try to be friendly), but occasionally I have had people persist in wanting to know it all. This is okay on short flights, but what about those five-hour hauls to the opposite coast or to Europe? I have heard that Dr. Hans Selye, the renowned stress expert, carries buds of raw garlic when he travels and eats them when he encounters an annoying seatmate. Raw garlic gives me heartburn. Can you suggest an alternative, short of being blatantly rude? B.G.*

Rather than finding it annoying, you should consider a captive audience a perfect opportunity to exercise your imagination. A friend of mine used to look forward to the tedious train trip she was required to take weekly as a chance to try different personae on for size. She has been, on different occasions, on her way to a torrid love affair with a major political figure, whose need for privacy required her to change trains three times; running away from a sheik who wished to include her in his harem; a brilliant research scientist escaping with a formula her unscrupulous supervisor wanted to claim as his own in order to win the Nobel Prize; and a society matron on her way to deposit ransom money for her kidnapped son in a locker at the end of the line. Most people regretted trying to engage her in conversation and, after five minutes, usually retreated into a paperback novel. I wonder why.

I'm really sorry to report that there is no guaranteed technique for dealing with a garrulous seatmate. When confronted with someone who thinks "non-stop" is an order, not a description of the itinerary, I can only suggest you look as preoccupied as possible by opening to page 114 of a murder mystery or catching up on some paperwork.

Do take time off from your misanthropy when meals are served — the French maintain that eating alone is bad for the digestion, and anyone who can balance a magazine in one hand while trying to eat off an airline tray with the other gets my annual Dexterity Above and Beyond Award with oak leaf cluster. For those of you who have wanted to talk to your seatmate but have kept silent because she has been buried in reading matter, here's your big chance. Offer to trade your salad, which you notice she's devoured, for the trifle she's left untouched. Offer to buy her a bottle of wine or to share the one you've already ordered. Making a pass while travelling is easier than in any other circumstances. For one thing, there's no moving to another bar stool if the plane or train is packed. For another, your motives are apparently innocent; you were going to Cleveland anyway. She is too, for that matter, so you already have something in common.

The most trivial observation will serve as a conversation starter (the train is delayed/on time; the inflight movie is wonderful/dreadful). However, if she immediately reaches into her briefcase for a file folder, you have no choice but to obey her wishes for privacy.

Dear Eve: *While on a plane recently, I was shocked when the woman in the seat next to me started applying her makeup a few minutes before we were to land. Is such behavior permissible? O.N.*

Most decidedly. While it would be undignified for milady to perform her *toilette* in public in any other situation, on board a plane it is highly encouraged. One doesn't need to tie up limited washroom facilities to add another coat of mascara after an overnight flight when everyone else is dying to brush their teeth and perform more immediate hygienic functions.

No matter where you go or how you plan to get there, all I ask of you, fellow travellers, is to keep the following words in mind as you set off for your destination: "The point, Eliza," wrote George Bernard Shaw, long before the pleasures and pitfalls of long journeys were a part of everyday life, "is not to have good manners or bad manners or any particular sort of manners, but having the same manners for all human souls; in short, behaving as though you were in Heaven where there are no third class carriages and one soul is as good as another."

CHAPTER TWELVE

To Insure Promptness

Some people are born tippers: a perfunctory glance at the bottom of the bill, out comes the wallet ever so casually, neat notes are piled on the platter (no cluttery quarters, no nickel-and-diming the process to death), the waiter beams and an appreciative chorus of thank-yous, come-agains, pleasure-to-serve-yous accompanies the departure of the gracious guest. Not me. I'm considering having a pocket calculator implant.

It's not just the addition and subtraction — and how many of us will be haunted forever by the specter of that lunch with the gang which ended up in a horrible row over who had the margarita — it's figuring out the logarithms of The Correct Percentage. "Ten" used to cover it, but these days, when standards have been revised to reflect the easy largesse of the corporate expense account, that's slumming it in a high class joint but still *de trop* in a greasy spoon; it might be acceptable at lunch but it's a crime against humanity at dinner. Things have become so complicated in the gratuities department that I sometimes wonder if anything short of an advanced degree in applied mathematics can give you the confidence necessary to go through the ordeal with anything approaching elegance.

Tipping has gotten vastly out of hand — it seems everywhere you turn there's one outstretched. Travel, for example, is fraught with all sorts of perils: one might crash, or find oneself in Yaoundé with a revolution brewing and no flights out till next Tuesday or, worst of all, occupy the seat next to a proud grandmother from Burlington who just happens to have a photo album handy in her flight bag. But these are mere trifles when compared to dealing with airport and train station porters. Trying to find out the going rate is like trying to find out the winning numbers in a ghetto racket. And what's the use of knowing it's fifty cents a bag at La Guardia if you've just disembarked at Palaam Airport in New Delhi? It's all so humiliating; not even a perfectly matched set of Hermès suitcases will save you when confronted with an upturned palm, the universal sign of welcome.

I once got off the train in London and, before I could get to the nearest bank to lay in a supply of the appropriate currency, I found myself face to face with an overly eager porter who was holding my luggage to ransom. I scraped together the few coppers I had in my possession from a previous trip as well as the odd Swiss franc and held them out to him as a peace offering. "Wot's dis 'ere, then?" he snarled as he took them from me. "I'm afraid it's all I have," I answered, feeling sheepish. He flung the coins back at me contemptuously, leaving me to lug my gear the length of Victoria Station. A valuable lesson, you'll agree, on the advantages of travelling light in possessions but heavy on the petty cash.

Consider, for a moment, the number of people one encounters who fully expect a bit above and beyond the stated amount for services rendered: caterers, locker room attendants, hotel maids, strolling musicians, shoeshine boys, hairdressers, doormen, taxi drivers, newspaper delivery boys, letter carriers (at Christmas, at least), parking garage jockeys, coat-check girls, all the personnel on a cruise ship, not to mention waiters and waitresses, bless their bunioned feet and damn their hungry eyes.

I feel I can safely ignore several of the above (especially the cruise ship crew, since I can't think of any way I'd rather spend my holidays less than to be held prisoner on a floating amusement park for weeks on end *and* have to bestow gratitude on my jailers) but there are far too many others who hold one's life — or one's car keys, mail, coat, take your pick — in the palms of their greedy little hands.

When I go on a business trip, I am meticulous about filling in my expense account sheet as soon as I return. And when I've added up the credit card receipts, hotel bills and cab slips, there's inevitably at least a twelve-dollar discrepancy between what they all come to and the amount I'm out of pocket. I've finally almost figured out just how that twelve dollars has slipped through my fingers: a dollar went to the bellboy for carrying my bags up to my room. The parking jockey bought a couple of beers with the two dollars in all I gave him (fifty cents each time he squealed the tires on my rented car in and out of the hotel garage). Five bucks was the very least I felt I owed the room service waiter after one of my guests had sent him up and down the elevator for, in chronological order, another glass, more ice, a cleaner glass, another bottle of whiskey (which she hardly needed) and, not a moment too soon, a pot of coffee.

The locker room attendant at the hotel pool got fifty cents from me when I went to soak my head to recover from the night before. I left two dollars on the pillow for the maid just before I checked out and handed the doorman a dollar for putting my bags into the cab to the airport as a final gesture. Twelve dollars is not that much in the greater scheme of the universe, I grant you, but when it goes, it's gone. (You math geniuses out there will notice there's still four bits unaccounted for. I told you I was no good at this and you didn't believe me. Ha!)

WILL THAT BE ALL, SIR?

Dear Eve: *There's a very chic restaurant in town where it's practically impossible to get a table. I've been there on several nights with a reservation and still have had to wait up to an hour to be seated. But I've seen people who have arrived later than me go into a huddle with the maitre d' and then be whisked off promptly into the dining room while the ice cubes in the drink I'm holding in the bar go right on melting. I have a feeling that they are tipping the maitre d' to get preferred treatment. I feel really naïve when this happens and have often wished I had enough cool to do it myself. But I've never actually seen money change hands and would have no idea how much to give the guy. Can you straighten me out? P.O'R.*

Slipping a maitre d' a fiver in order to secure a table is not a tip — it is a bribe. For those of you who wish to indulge in such dubious practices, go right ahead, see if I care. I'll just wait quietly until my table of choice is available, or go elsewhere.

The restaurant you describe may indeed be very chic, but it is obviously not very good. Restaurants are in business to provide two things: food and service. Any establishment that keeps a customer waiting for up to an hour despite reservations falls grievously short in the latter category. If they cannot honor a commitment made over the telephone, I'll wager a dinner at Maxim's that the filet with herbed butter advertised on their menu is chuck steak with parsley and margarine.

I am always amazed at the degree of humiliation people will put up with in order to be seen in the "right" place. There's a classy joint not far from my house which is famous as a hangout for celebrities. The food is superb, the atmosphere charming, but the true beauty of the place is that you can show up there at one in the morning in a scruffy pair of jeans and they'll treat you like somebody. You might indeed be nobody but they're not taking any chances that you don't have enough money in your bank account to buy the place out if the spirit moves you. A noted (and extremely powerful) food critic, who safeguards her anonymity the way medieval maidens used to safeguard their chastity, makes a point of looking like a mouse when she visits a restaurant for the first time. Later, in print, she shows no mercy if she's seated by the kitchen door, ignored for twenty minutes after she has closed the menu, or bypassed when she wants a drink of water by a waiter on his way to fawn over a toney crew that's just walked in. The world's creamiest chocolate mousse won't save the place when she sits down to write her review.

Tips are a gesture of appreciation. This restaurant does not seem to appreciate having you as a customer, so I don't see why you should be so eager to pay for the privilege of being abused.

DEAR EVE: *I always settle the bill in a restaurant with a waiter and leave a tip for him, but I have often wondered if this is the right thing to do. The maitre d', the bartender and the busboys also provide service, and I would guess they need the extra cash too. Is it proper to give them something after a fine meal and, if so, how much? C.N.M.*

Hey, big spender, you've done your bit. The tokens of your esteem will find their way to the appropriate pockets when you tip the server. It is his responsibility to make sure the other members of the staff get their due. Fifteen per cent, which really is the minimum at any place with real tablecloths, is usually broken up according to some arcane formula that has been arrived at by management as the fairest way of divvying up the take. There is, however, nothing preventing you from upping the ante if the waiter has been waltzing around all night picking tomatoes out of the salad because your companion is allergic to them. Not only is there nothing preventing you, you really should. The chef gets nothing, except your compliments if they are deserved.

If you frequent a place often enough so that they know to make up a salad *sans* tomatoes the minute you walk in the door, it doesn't hurt to let the maitre d' know his dive has a special place in your heart. After the sixth or seventh visit, tender a note to him on your way out and say, "George, this is for all the fine service I've been getting, thanks to you. It's always a pleasure to come back." Bring your boss on your next visit because, with any luck, they'll really be puttin' on the Ritz for your benefit and he or she will be appropriately impressed.

DEAR EVE: *How much do you leave at a restaurant coat-check? P.D.*

These damsels (as they so often are) in the doorway can be quite distressing unless you learn their language: whatever amount is displayed in the saucer is usually the amount that is expected of you. Don't be daunted by a mountain of quarters — it simply means they are the preferred coinage of the realm. Add at least one per coat if you are travelling in a pack; two per if it's just you and a friend. Some places are enlightened enough to post a sign informing customers of the going rate and that settles that.

MY WIFE DOESN'T UNNERSHTAND ME

DEAR EVE: *I can handle figuring out a tip from the amount at the bottom of a bill, but what do you do at a stand-up bar where you're expected to pay after every drink? Should you tip each time or leave something when you're ready to go? Can you fill me in on the proper procedure? W.H.*

Sure can. Belly up to the bar, boys, and watch this. Practised drinkers announce their presence by laying a five- or ten-dollar bill on the bar before giving the order. This signals to the barkeep that they intend to warm the bar stools or polish up the foot rail for a while, and he shouldn't forget them after just one beer.

When the first round arrives, the barman takes his due out of the money in front of you and leaves the change on the counter.

Push a quarter, at least, in his direction before he goes off to tend to other customers. Add to the pile as you drink your way through it, a bit for him, a bit for you, until you've had enough or have liquidated all your assets. If there's nothing but change on the bar when you're ready to leave, it's good form to leave it there as an overall token of gratitude.

There's no fixed percentage for over-the-counter service. A handful of loose change is considered equitable, except if you're running a tab. Then you should add the standard fifteen percent when it comes time to settle. *Pousse-cafés* are an art, not a drink, so show your admiration for a steady hand. And if you insist on bending the bartender's ear with tales of woe, at least offer to buy him a drink — it's a better deal than psychoanalysis.

IF MUSIC BE THE FOOD OF LOVE

DEAR EVE: *Muzak is bad enough, but more and more restaurants are providing musical acompaniment for the meals they serve. Wine is plenty for me, but my girlfriend goes into swoons of rapture when she gets ersatz gypsy love songs served up with her pasta. What are you supposed to do when a roving guitarist picks your table to pluck a few strings? More importantly, are you supposed to tip him? M.F.*

It's enough to make you want to slink into the nearest dimly lit bar where it's quite safe to ignore the piano-man off in his little corner, letting you get on with your Rob Roy in peace. (If you like what he's up to, you can always send him a drink with your compliments. But watch it — too many of those will cause him to break into "I Did It My Way" and then you'll be sorry.)

Unless the man with the flying fingers is Segovia and his visit falls between courses, keep eating but stop talking; pay him the courtesy of listening if nothing else. If you like what you hear or have requested a special number ("If you can play it for her, you can play it for me, Sam. Play it again" is the way it goes), you may choose to — but you're not obliged to — show tangible appreciation. But don't do it then and there. When the waiter comes by with the bill, hand him an extra dollar or two and inform him it's for the musician. Or hand it to him yourself on your way out the door, if he's not busy strumming his heart out for someone else. The point of all restaurant maneuvers is to avoid fumbling with your wallet until you've finished your filet of sole. Greasy bills are rarely appreciated, no matter what their denomination.

TRAVEL TIPS

DEAR EVE: *Aside from the fact that I never know why I'm tipping the taxi driver — he doesn't open my door, and it certainly isn't for his scintillating conversation — I never seem to know how much to give. What is fair: the loose change or a definite percentage? D.C.G.*

Loose change is certainly more practical when you have to struggle with shopping bags, get out your housekeys and step into oncoming traffic all at the same time, but if the loose change is all that's left of $6.00 when the meter reads $5.90, you're going to look rather cheap, and the Fates will be on the cabbie's side when you catch your sleeve in the door handle and drop your parcels all over the curb.

A tip of 15 to 20 percent applies on long hauls, such as to the airport. When luggage is put into and taken out of the trunk, most cabs will charge a certain amount per bag in addition to the metered fare. This should be clearly posted inside the car. For short hops around town, try to keep at least a quarter handy to supplement whatever loose change you have coming to you.

DEAR EVE: *I never know what to do about the airline crew when getting off a plane. Are you supposed to tip them? I've never seen anyone do this but maybe people give them a gratuity when I'm not paying attention. Could you straighten me out? J.L.*

Ah, the crew. Rodney Dangerfield gets more respect than they do. They've heard every joke ever invented (twice), fended off more passes than an NHL goalie, given thousands of safety demonstrations when no one was paying the slightest bit of attention (one stewardess was so exasperated at being ignored, she placed the oxygen mask over her left breast instead of over her nose and mouth and no one blinked). They've handed out a pharmacy's worth of aspirin, cleaned up after too many passengers who think the sign above the toilet sink is just there for decoration, run countless Boston Marathons up and down the aisles trying to keep everyone's coffee cup filled and broken up more fights than a boxing referee. ("Miss, tell that man to stop bothering me." "What's he doing, ma'am?" "Just tell him to stop." "I can't tell him to stop if I don't know what it is you want stopped." "I'll whisper it ... See that sombrero on his lap? He's got nothing on under it!")

And yet, and yet ... the only thing you must *not* do on a flight is tip them. A refreshing change, wouldn't you agree? The reason for this is simple: airplane crews are not technically service personnel. In the early days of commercial air travel, the cabin was staffed by trained nurses, and even today, the average attendant is more concerned with first aid than which wine goes with what. To offer a gratuity is an insult to their sense of professionalism. Besides, most companies prohibit them from taking tips unless the passenger insists to the point of causing a row. Tips that are accepted in these cases are often turned over to a charity.

The only thing you are required to do is return the crew's farewells on your way out. They've worked damn hard to make your trip as pleasant as possible, and you'd be surprised how hurt they can be if you avoid their eyes and try to slink out without so much as a simple thank you.

THE PRICE PAID FOR BEAUTY

The fellow who does my hair used to do Dolly Parton's wigs. So, at the end of an hour at his mercy, I usually feel I owe him something for the inside dope on Her Excessiveness and for resisting the urge to relive his former glory at the expense of my less than Grand Ol' Opry head. Come to think of it, I'm incredibly grateful he leaves me looking like me, only more so.

A visit to the beauty salon is one of life's great luxuries; it's as close as most of us will ever come to knowing what it's like to have a ladies' maid or valet. If Madame de Sévigné were alive today, she'd have to revise her famous dictum to: "No man is a hero to his hairstylist." Even less of a hero if he doesn't leave a proper tip.

DEAR EVE: *I'm always at a loss when it comes to who gets what at a hairdresser's. I've been told it is in bad taste to tip the proprietor when he or she cuts your hair. Is this true? G.J.*

Your sources are quite correct. The prerogatives of owning the shop include picking and choosing the heads one will deign to beautify and charging for the honor. But knowing the score is a bit tricky. If you draw Henri on a visit to *Henri le Coiffeur*, you can be pretty sure the bill will come to a bit more than the advertised rate, and that Henri will shake his head and murmur, "*Mais ce n'est pas nécessaire*" when you reach into your wallet to express your gratitude. But if you visit an establishment known as *Les Trois Colombes*, you have no way of knowing whether the young woman massaging henna into your scalp is one of the doves in question. When you're not sure who's who in the cast, be prepared to tip, but also be prepared to smile and offer a simple thank-you when your gesture is met with a "*mais ce n'est pas ...*"

Mere employees must never be neglected. Many stylists work on commission, not on salary, and every little bit helps. The fellow who trims your tresses should get between two and four dollars on a twenty dollar haircut, depending on how satisfied you are with the results. You can slip it into his pocket just before you leave, unless he's wearing incredibly tight jeans and you don't want to get that personal. A more tactful method in such circumstances would be to leave it at his station, tucked under a hairbrush. A dollar or so should go to the person who shampooed your hair, if different from the above.

Even if your beautifying ritual is a mammoth production that calls for a cast of thousands (manicurist, eyelash tinter, leg waxer, moustache clipper and I can't for the life of me imagine who else), they all deserve a mention when the credits roll. Enter the premises armed with singles and, by the time they're through with you, you'll feel lighter than air. Not only will you look better, your wallet won't be weighing you down.

WHAT — NO ANCHOVIES?

Dear Eve: *Is one expected to tip the person who delivers pizza? I feel that tipping, like unions, has got out of control. K.T.*

If the people who deliver pizzas had unions, you wouldn't need to ask this question. They would have the collective strength to seek a living wage and you wouldn't have to subsidize their incomes and help to keep down their employers' overhead.

It's a lousy job, but somebody's got to do it. If you are confronted, as I have been, with a frostbitten soul who has braved 20 below zero weather in a car without a heater *and* managed to produce a dinner redolent of sunny Italy, have a heart. I agree we have to draw the line somewhere, but the pizza delivery boy is not the place to start. What did he ever do to you? Pick out all the anchovies en route?

Be grateful you don't live in France where you have to slip a franc each to innumerable usherettes for the privilege of finding your own seat in a darkened movie theater and where the entrances to public toilets are guarded by Gorgons who, having survived the men who gave their all for la République during World War II, are awarded the right to sit in the doorways with their little white saucers and reign as "*les dames pipi*." We have neither of these glorious institutions here, but then they don't have take-out pizza.

CHAPTER THIRTEEN

Home 0, Visitors 7

One of the hazards of living in a large metropolitan area and being the friendly sort, especially the friendly sort who is the proud possessor of that most unspeakable of urban luxuries, the spare bedroom, is that word gets out. I have so many people passing through in need of a place to stay it's no coincidence my place is known as The Greta Garbo Home for Wayward Boys and Girls. Boyfriends of the moment have been known to send cables in desperation to inform me that they are available once the crowd has dispersed.

Some houseguests — such as the old college chum who always arrives with a small gift, insists on making at least one meal for me while she's visiting and leaves the spare bedroom neater than she found it — are a pure delight, and I usually can't wait until they show up again. Others — such as the job-hunting son of parents' friends who phoned Passaic, New Jersey three times (Passaic?!) without informing me, and whose only words to me before barricading himself in the bathroom at 8 a.m. were, "Let me know when breakfast is ready" — would be well-advised to know that the Hav-A-Nap Motel's rates are quite reasonable.

The French have their *crimes passionnels*, but I maintain that speaking to me in the morning before I've finished reading the paper is grounds for justifiable homicide. Visitors (have pity on their temporarily homeless souls) must be prepared to defer to their host's quirks at all times. The price for a rent-free roof over one's head while on the road is invisibility. This may sound terribly harsh, but I have been a visitor as often as I have been a visitee and have found that barely having been there is the surest guarantee of being invited back.

THIS WAY TO YOUR ROOM, SIR

Dear Eve: *An out-of-town friend called me a while ago and asked if I would mind putting up someone he knows at my apartment for a few days. There's plenty of room, and I don't in the least mind doing this friend a favor, so I agreed. I know this person is coming to do business, not just to visit me, but I'm wondering how much I need to do for him. I am a very busy person and don't want to have to set time aside for a relative stranger, but I don't want to appear inhospitable either. Is it enough to give him a set of spare keys and tell him to make himself at home? H.W.*

If you merely tell him to make himself at home, you might discover, to your chagrin, that his idea of home is to down an entire bottle of Courvoisier, turn up the stereo so loud that the next-door neighbor takes to pounding the wall, leave dirty dishes in the sink and scatter his clothes all over the living room floor. I know whereof I speak: one cannot simply take someone else's upbringing for granted. I suggest you plan to be home for at least the first evening for an orientation session. This means laying down some ground rules in a way that suggests you are trying to help him navigate around your territory to everyone's convenience.

For the first night, anyway, make up the spare bed or sofa yourself with clean linen. Now that we're all grown up, crashing on the floor should be a thing of the past; our tired old bones demand a more peaceful rest, especially on a business trip. If your guest will be occupying center stage in the major thoroughfare of your home, warn him of the hour you intend to be passing through. The most obvious hint that you find an unmade bed in your living room an eyesore is precise instructions on how the thing folds up and which cushions go where when the damn thing isn't doing cot duty. Provide him with a towel, give him a rundown of your habits ("I need the bathroom at around eight; there's coffee in the third cabinet on the right when you walk into the kitchen and grapefruit in the fridge; please help yourself") and explain that your busy schedule means he will have to be responsible for himself.

To make him feel a little less as though he's only there on sufferance, you might want to add a few considerate touches: leave a map of the city's transportation system and a list of the best restaurants or the day's newspaper open to the entertainment page next to his bed. Who knows? He might prove to be such a civilized guest that you'll want to get to know him the next time he comes to town.

YOU'LL NOTICE THERE'S NO FRONT DESK, FOR ONE THING

As a guest, you must never ever confuse a private home with a hotel. In case you can't tell the difference, look for these telltale signs: a hotel provides maid service, most private homes do not; a hotel's kitchen may function twenty-four hours a day, allowing you to have breakfast at noon and dinner at 2 a.m., a private home's does not; a hotel might be delighted you've decided to entertain a newly acquired friend on its premises, a private home will not be. There is, however, one thing a hotel and a private home have in common: neither maintains an open bar.

DEAR EVE: *In my business, I meet people from all over, and they inevitably say things like, "If you're ever in Winnipeg, you must come and stay with us." I never know if they mean it. Well, it just so happens, I am planning to go to Winnipeg soon, and I wouldn't mind getting to know the peope I met from there. How can I find out if their invitation is for real? R.S.*

Depending on how much time you have before you go, either write or call ahead of time (you'd be calling to make hotel reservations anyway, so don't save a buck or two if time is short). Remind them who you are and where you met; even though you might think the invitation was issued because you made such a great impression, they might be the promiscuous sort who think nothing of putting out the welcome mat for any potential stray. Tell them what you've just told me: you're going to be in Winnipeg, you'd like to see them again and did they really mean it when they said there's always an extra bed? It's really very simple.

But once you're there, remember that the boundary between being a guest and being a freeloader is a very fine one, and you must be careful not to cross it, especially if you're hoping to be back in Winnipeg one day. A guest is someone who adds something to the household or at least doesn't drastically diminish the existing stock. A guest goes to the corner for milk when he has emptied the last drop into his coffee, replaces books and records on the shelf where he found them, livens up the dinner table with a bouquet of flowers or contributes a bottle of wine to the evening meal. Being a stranger in a city is no excuse: it's as easy to ask if there's a liquor store nearby as it is to find out where the nearest bank or post office is. Arriving without a gift in hand is forgivable, leaving without any show of gratitude is not.

DEAR EVE: *Friends arrived not too long ago with their two kids. We were not only expected to babysit, but also to cook the kids' favorite foods (they are really picky eaters). How can we get it across to them that we are not in the kiddie care business? L.C.*

Situations such as this give me the urge to plant a "For Sale" sign on the front lawn and leave without a forwarding address. Why do people abuse others' hospitality so?

Your responsibility as a host for a package tour which includes kids ends with providing beds and perhaps stocking up on peanut butter and alphabet soup. But expecting you to spend all your time tending to your junior visitors is, shall we say, presumptuous.

Give Mom and Dad the usual grand tour and offer to liberate the kitchen at a set time so that they can see to Tad and Muffy's supper themselves. If they announce they have theater tickets that evening, say "What a coincidence. We were planning to go to the movies," and hand them the phone number of a local babysitter.

If children disrupt your life to the degree that you've described, next time I hope you'll know better than to invite guests *en famille*.

WAS THAT A SINGLE OR A DOUBLE YOU RESERVED?

All that I've said so far makes it sound as though the onus for a trouble-free visit sits squarely with the guest. That is not entirely the case. A host has his share of responsibilities. Besides the three Bs —

bed, breakfast and bathing facilities (which include towels and soap) — be prepared to make allowances for a guest's faulty memory. In a pinch, you should be able to provide a toothbrush, an alarm clock, a needle and thread and even stationery.

The one thing you absolutely must not do is run your guest ragged. No matter how many marvelous museums your city boasts and no matter how great your belief in the benefit of calisthenics first thing in the morning, let the poor sod set his own pace, or he'll be recuperating on your day bed for far longer than you had intended him to stay.

DEAR EVE: *We have been married for less than a year and have always lived in the same town as my parents. Several months ago, my husband got a hurried promotion and we find ourselves in a city where lodging is hard to come by. As a result, we are living in a tiny one-bedroom apartment. The problem is that my parents are coming out for a visit, and I feel we should give them our bed. My husband says they would not expect this and thinks it's enough to put them on the fold-out couch in the living-dining-room. What do you say? S.R.*

I say nothing tests the mettle more than cramped quarters, and nothing cramps the quarters more than having one's parents come to stay. They are the only people you should consider liberating your bed for. Having your own double bed is probably the reason you left home in the first place, but Mom and Dad should never have to put up with the indignity of not having a door to close against the cat's morning ministrations. Do remember to unhook the trapeze from the ceiling before they arrive.

Other couples, married or otherwise, must make the best of the accommodations available. They'll just have to forgo their conjugal duties if the best hospitality you can muster does not include a double bed. But Mom and Dad are in a category all their own, and I recommend you make the supreme sacrifice.

DEAR EVE: *I own a cottage on a lake, which I try to get up to most weekends. Since I've bought it, I've become very popular with my downtown friends. But that's okay — I like company and most of them are considerate enough to come equipped with a case of beer or some other contribution of food or drink.*

The place is fairly large and I can accommodate at least two other couples quite comfortably. I've furnished it with small double beds because most people I know come in pairs. My question is this: I have a very good friend who is gay. He asked me recently if he could come for a visit. That's fine by me, but he wants to bring a friend. I've given it a lot of thought and finally decided that if my heterosexual friends are allowed to bring companions, there's no reason why he shouldn't be too. But I don't know whether to assume that they're going to share a bed. How should I handle the situation? B.G.

You should welcome them as you would any other couple. If you are not going to be comfortable with the idea of the two of them sleeping together, you had no business inviting them up in the first place. It sounds as though you have made your peace with your friend's sexual preferences, but I guess the sleeping arrangements are a bit bothersome, just as they are with parents who know their unmarried children are sexually active but don't want it confirmed under their own roof.

An acquaintance of mine found himself in a situation not unlike yours a while ago. He decided he wouldn't be embarrassed if his guests slept together, but he wasn't sure that they wouldn't be embarrassed by his assumption they were going to sleep together. Not wanting to take any chances, he made up two beds and, when they arrived, gave them a tour of the premises, pointing out that two bedrooms were at their disposal. The visitors looked at each other, grinned, and finally one said to him: "No point messing up two beds, is there?" And the matter was closed.

LONG DISTANCE CALLING

Telephones and visitors are a lethal combination. Your in-for-the-weekend girlfriend might moan and groan about missing her husband, but you won't know how much she missed him till the phone bill arrives a month after she's gone. Short of installing a pay phone in the vestibule, you are bound to receive these mementos of otherwise delightful visits from time to time.

Mindful of not abusing others as I have been abused, I always ask permission before using the phone when being billeted, and reverse the charges or bill the call to my home number whenever possible.

If you must call directly for whatever reason, I suggest you slip a five dollar bill under the receiver before you leave the premises. If your call costs less, your host will owe you and you'll have a reason to return.

DEAR EVE: *If you're staying in someone's house and your host isn't there, should you answer the telephone? R.P.*

Yes. For one thing, the ringing will drive you crazy if you don't. For another, it might be for you. (I assume you aren't hiding from the police or a jealous husband and have notified your loved ones of your whereabouts.)

A simple "Hello" will suffice. Please don't give into the temptation to be overly formal and pick up the receiver with a Jeeves-ish "McGinty residence." That truly belongs to a bygone era. If it's for your host, ask if you can take a message. Don't volunteer any information about where he is or when he is due to return — it might be his boss wondering why he's not at the office or yet another jealous husband. If it's for you, well, carry on.

THE SPIRIT OF ALEXANDER WOOLCOTT LIVES ON

DEAR EVE: *How do you get rid of The Man Who Came to Dinner? I've had a houseguest for far too long now, and he doesn't seem inclined to decamp. Originally, he asked me if he could stay at my place till he found one of his own, but I think he has come to the conclusion my place is his own. W.T.*

Well, George S. Kaufman and Moss Hart couldn't figure out a way of getting him to leave when they wrote their play more than forty years ago, and I don't know that any progress has been made since. You can try rigging a neon "Exit" sign over the front door or leaving the Apartments To Let section of the classifieds lying around where he's most likely to trip over it, but I don't honestly believe the human race, in all its ingeniousness, has ever devised anything better to solve the problem than the simple statement, "I think it's time for you to go."

In your efforts to spare his feelings, you've probably made him so comfortable that he's immune to diplomacy, deaf to veiled entreaties and blind to the havoc he's causing. And he's lost the urge to seek shelter elsewhere. There's no beating around the bush on this one — you either ask him to leave point blank, or you get used to setting a place at table for one more.

The cardinal rule of being a houseguest, as you seem to be aware, is not to overstay your welcome. An invitation for the weekend is just that. Monday morning should find you nothing more than a pleasant memory. The cardinal rule of being a host, on the other hand, is to let your guests know exactly how long their presence will be tolerated. I know from painful personal experience that the guest who arrives in July and is still around in September might not realize that temporary tenancy at The Greta Garbo Home is limited to two weeks. After that, one is expected to pay rent. (The bounder stayed on, but my cat packed her bags and split, so the population remained stable.) Sit your friend down and say, "Sandy, this is really a very small apartment and I'm not used to sharing it with anyone. I'm glad to help a friend out occasionally, but in return I expect the friend to be as sensitive to my needs as I have been to his." Vamoose, kid, amscray ... shoo!

AND DON'T COME BACK

Dear Eve: *While I was staying with some friends, I had a small accident. There was a little china horse on the dresser in the room where I was sleeping, and I managed to knock it over and break it. I put the pieces in a drawer and left without saying anything, but now I feel really guilty. Should I do something about it? A.R.*

Yes. 'Fess up. You have no idea of the extent of your transgression and, chances are, it's going to bother you a lot more than it's worth. For all you know, the broken trinket was something Uncle Wilbur dragged home from The Wars, the demise of which is entirely welcome. People tend to put *objets* of less than *l'art* in places they are not likely to be seen too often, such as the spare bedroom.

However, just in case this was a treasure of the T'ang dynasty, better your hosts should know that you're clumsy than suspect you of pocketing it. If you haven't already written your thank-you letter, I recommend you do so now, including what you have just told me near the end (the old first-the-good-news gambit). Offer to have the horse repaired if possible, replaced if necessary. Pray they bought it at Woolworth's.

CHAPTER FOURTEEN

Friendships

Their Care and Feeding

Just as there is no sound in outer space (or so I hear), there is no etiquette without other people. We are polite or rude only in relation to the folks who have to put up with us, day in and day out.

Formality is the first line of defense in unfamiliar situations with unfamiliar people. Many of my correspondents are primarily concerned with not making utter fools of themselves in public. But behind closed doors, it's another story. I have had the misfortune to get to know people who, on first impression, were the epitome of urbanity. But the same elegant fellow whose reputation for making maitre d's swoon in delight extends to three cities, to my horror, turned out to be the sort who burps by way of good morning, stubs his cigarettes out in the philodendron and leaves cold pizza slices scattered around the living room floor in homage to some minor deity who did not figure in the pantheon of those of us who happened to share a house with him. We were blessed, he never ceased to inform us, because he loved us all so much he felt he could drop the "pretense" he feels obliged to maintain in the company of those who matter less to him. Thanks for the honor. I think.

Intimacy is not license. Just because you've known someone for years or happen to be blood relations is no reason to dispense with the courtesies you would extend to anyone else.

YOURS SINCERELY

In one of his thoughtful essays in *Esquire* magazine, Harry Stein used an interesting statistic as evidence that the care and feeding of friendships is in sad decline. To wit:

> There was a time when separation used to add a new dimension to friendships, the exchange of letters revealing quirks or charms or insights never grasped face to face; the state of human relations has deteriorated so obviously in this regard that it *can* be measured in government reports.
>
> According to the [U.S.] Postal Service ... about 80 percent of today's first-class mail is business related, and of the remaining 20 percent, fully 17 percent is given over to greeting cards and other expressions of sentiment by proxy.

Can you imagine the loss to literary history (not to mention the gain to his masculinity) if Abelard had sent Heloise seventy-five-cent Snoopy valentines instead of his poetic declarations of passion? Manners (and politics for that matter) would never have progressed to their current dizzying heights if Lord Chesterfield hadn't thought to give his son a few pointers about carrying on in the company of dukes and duchesses in a series of letters which were passed on to posterity. And the Corinthians would probably have gone right on wallowing in sin if St. Paul hadn't dashed off a few epistles advising them to keep on the straight and narrow.

Correspondence, in fact, was taken so seriously not too long ago that a stationery wardrobe (no, it isn't a closet that stands still ... learn to spell) was as vital to the calling of lady or gentleman as were kid gloves with three pearl buttons at the wrist. Oh sure, there are still a few female denizens of wealthy suburbs who possess large stocks of stippled blue notepaper with their monogram embossed in white on the front and on the flap of the matching envelope, but how many of us keep black-bordered paper for mourning on hand? Or are aware that cream double sheets with a burgundy monogram are appropriate for personal letters, while single white sheets with an address engraved in black are reserved for business? Admit it — you didn't know there were rules like this and you've frankly never cared. Today, we all have dialing fingers instead of calling cards, and answering services have taken the place of butlers. Some wag has suggested that the great literature of the future will have titles such as *The Collected Phone Messages of Norman Mailer*. Sigh.

DEAR EVE: *I'm at my wit's end and patience's end when it comes to my best friend who, a year ago, moved to the west coast. She loves her new home and thanks to family friction has no plans to come back here even for a visit. She also doesn't write or phone. I'm reduced to relying on garbled secondhand news of her through letters of a mutual friend out there.*

She pleads student poverty for not phoning or visiting, but the cost of a stamp would hardly break her budget. I've begged, pleaded, even stopped my long, frequent letters to her in an attempt to improve her correspondence but nothing works. We love each other and long to stay in touch, but I'm really annoyed that I'll have to spend a couple of hundred dollars to fly out there if I really want to hear her news. How can I convince her to pick up that pen? F.F.

You can't. Being the Maxwell Perkins of the epistolary world is singularly unsatisfying. If the dear girl can't or won't write, well, the dear girl can't or won't write. She might be made to talk, however, if the love and longing to stay in touch are as great as you say. (I have only your word for it; her actions are evidence to the contrary.)

This is the electronic age, after all, and there are all sorts of marvelous devices available to transmit one's thoughts over great distances without enriching the phone company's coffers. Is it real or is it Memorex? If she is as poor as she says she is, why not send her a small tape recorder as a gift? Not only will she have a fine memento of your affection, she might be inspired to speak into it on occasion and send you the end result. It should cost less than a plane ticket but enough to make her feel guilty.

PLEASE, THANK YOU AND I'M SORRY

INTERNATIONAL NEWS FLASH: Radio Tokyo reports, with considerable consternation, that Western manners have permeated Japanese society to the extent that its younger members no longer know how to bow correctly. But never fear; as the inhabitants of the island empire have demonstrated time and again, where there's a will, there's an appropriate technology. To deal with this dreaded decline in decorum, the folks who gave us the talking car (proving life *does* imitate television) have created a computer capable of teaching the disrespectful young'uns the correct stance for paying obeisance to their elders and betters.

It works something like this: a young man pays his respects to the machine as best he knows how. A laser scans the topography of his spine, and a simulated female voice coaxes him to bend lower until the perfect posture is achieved. Would the honored gentlemen who invented this delightful device do me an enormous favor and develop a software package for "please," "thank you" and "I'm sorry" for the North American market?

"Please," "thank you" and "I'm sorry" are the three most ill-used expressions in the English language. (Neither "I love you" nor "We are working for peace" falls under the mandate of manners, so we'll just ignore them, shall we?) I know an adorable little old lady — the description is meant to be vivid, not patronizing — who walks into a room and immediately apologizes. All who know and love her are then left to speculate whether they were early and she is late, whether she ate all the goodies on her way through the kitchen or whether she inadvertently ran over the cat when she pulled into the driveway. After years of finding her not guilty of all these possible crimes, we've finally figured out she is apologizing for her mere existence. This is an incorrect usage: one should only say "I'm sorry" when one has done something for which one is to blame. I would therefore like to ask her publicly to cease and desist. You know who you are.

As for "please" and "thank you," there aren't nearly enough of them around. There is the case of the London souvenir shopkeeper who, upon not having what his customer wanted, was shocked by the tourist's silent acceptance of the situation and yelled, "Say 'thank you' or I'll bash your bloody head in!" But that's a British example, and the British are extreme in these matters.

DEAR EVE: *A very dear friend of mine had a baby some months ago. I sent her a rather nice present and expected a formal thank-you note. I'm still waiting. Another friend said I'm wrong to expect a thank-you note from someone that close. To top off my bad feelings, the new mother called recently to find out why I hadn't been in touch since she'd had the baby. I hemmed and hawed and pleaded guilty to all sorts of charges. What do you think I should have done? J.W.*

I think your friend owes you both thanks and an apology. As for whether you should hold out for one, the other or both in writing, perhaps you might agree to hold off on that for a moment and concentrate instead on reducing this mountain to the molehill it originally was. It sounds as though everyone concerned is overreacting.

You realize, of course, you blew your golden opportunity by not putting it straight to your friend when she phoned. But it's never too late. Get back on the phone to her and say, as simply and straightforwardly as possible, "I'm mad at you for not having acknowledged my gift." If she doesn't say "thank you" and "I'm sorry" in short order, consider her a former friend.

DEAR EVE: *Could you settle an argument my boyfriend and I are having? We were invited to dinner at his parents' house (I was meeting them for the first time) and afterwards I wanted to send them a thank-you letter. He said they are very informal people and that it was not the right thing to do. I didn't send one and now I feel odd about it. K.G.*

I've heard of lots of people who were upset because they didn't receive a thank-you, but I've never heard of anyone who was upset because they did. There is no such thing as being too gracious. I'm on your side.

DEAR EVE: *I recently had my name imprinted on some postcard-size stationery with matching envelopes. When is it correct to use them? Should I use them as thank-yous for functions which I attend alone, or can they be used by both my husband and me — for example, John and I would like to thank you for... L.D.P.*

Judging by your description, you've laid in a supply of "informals" and, as the name implies, they are to be used on any occasion of a lesser magnitude than a sit-down dinner at the family manor in honor of a visiting head of state, a debutante ball or a wedding. By all means use them for thank-yous. (Someone who still writes thank-yous! May you be blessed with a pen that never runs out of ink and a thousand return engagements!)

Even if only your name figures on the stationery, it would be appropriate to thank someone on your husband's behalf as well. Traditionally, women were entirely responsible for all social correspondence, even to the extent that wives who didn't know each other extended invitations on behalf of husbands who did. This, like so many other things, is changing, but the protocol-minded still hold that, on paper, you are the voice of your household.

Yours should be the only signature at the bottom, which means a Christian name and a surname. If your surname is different from your husband's for professional or other reasons and your friends only know you by your married name, print Mrs. John Suchandsuch beneath your signature in parentheses. Your husband, as you already seem to know, exists only in the third person for written purposes.

DEAR EVE: *Should one acknowledge a thank-you letter? L.J.*

No, it's so rare to get one that I can understand your urge to shout your gratitude from the rooftops. But enough's enough. If you send a thank-you letter in response to a thank-you letter, you might get a thank-you for your thank-you for your thank-you back. There's no point in overdoing things. Should you be speaking to the person who sent it, mention in passing how pleased you were to receive it. Then send a birthday card or a Christmas card or whatever other form of communication is next on the list of scheduled events. We've got to keep the Post Office on its toes.

DEAR EVE: *Recently I commited an egregious faux pas with my lady friend; to make amends, I sent her some flowers. She loved them and eventually everything got back to normal. But something is still bothering me. Although she agreed the flowers were nice, the gesture seemed to me desperately old-fashioned. Is there a more imaginative way to do these things? P.McD.*

Old-fashioned perhaps, but so rare as to be utterly delightful. A random survey among my female friends revealed that the last time most women received flowers from a man, except for when they were in the hospital, was the corsage they wore to the senior prom. *Où sont les fleurs d'antan*?

I can't think of anything better to give in such circumstances. If you want to be imaginative about it, stay away from the hackneyed (and expensive) red roses and maidenhair fern. Take a leaf from poor, mad Ophelia: "There's rosemary, that's for remembrance; pray love, remember; and there's pansies, that's for thoughts." I don't believe many florists stock rue, which would have been the most appropriate in your case, but irises or violets (blue flowers signify loyalty) would have gotten your message across nicely.

KISS AND MAKE UP

DEAR EVE: *Toward the end of a dinner party given by a pair of close friends, the host and hostess entered into an argument over what appeared to be a relatively trivial matter. The dispute rapidly escalated into a pitched battle over such less-than-trivial matters as the disputants' personal and moral characters and the general worthiness of each partner as a spouse. The eight guests who remained at that hour, including three who were to stay overnight, quickly abandoned the kitchen to the combatants and retired so as to be out of hearing range.*

We were embarrassed by the scene and made more uncomfortable by our ignorance as to what should be done. Does the ideal guest attempt to intervene, as we certainly would have done had the violence been physical rather than psychological? Should one simply retreat and hope it ends soon? Has one license to leave, and if so, is the departing guest obliged to enter the battlefield to thank the hosts for what had been, until then, a pleasant evening? And if one has contracted to stay the night, is it licit to try to find more hospitable quarters? If it isn't, how is one to behave at breakfast? K.M.

We'll take it as a given that your hosts were being incredibly inconsiderate, not only to each other, but also to the assembled company. You were not, after all, invited as a United Nations peacekeeping mission, you were asked to dinner. You did the right thing by withdrawing from the line of fire and, if that was the extent of your actions, no one could fault you for improper behavior. But since you say these are close friends, you would still have been well within the bounds of propriety if you had tried to get them to stop. Offering thanks for the evening as you left would not only have been polite for the usual reasons, it might have made them realize they were driving their guests away and brought them to their senses.

If their warring state was of more concern than your own feelings of discomfort, one of you might have asked to speak to the husband in private and another one to the wife, first as a way of breaking up the fight, and second as a way of letting them know you care without embarrassing them in front of everyone.

As for the captive audience, among the five of you who had homes to go to, I'm sure one or two could have offered alternative lodgings until the storm blew over. Sometimes it's easier to extend kindness to strangers than to friends.

GIVE AND TAKE

Whoever said "Tis better to give than to receive" was a bit off the mark. 'Tis not better, 'tis easier. If you're giving, all you have to do is figure out what the intended recipient needs, how much to spend and what color ribbon to tie it up with. Small potatoes. But for those who spend their lives considering themselves unworthy of any show of esteem, a gift freely given strikes terror in the heart.

To counteract this instinctive awkwardness, we, clever people that we are, have come up with the concept of social debt, otherwise known as The Tit for Tat School of Human Relations. But we're so bloody dishonest about it that we try to pretend otherwise and as a result, gifts become debts and debts become gifts and everybody goes around feeling like they've got the short end of the stick.

DEAR EVE: *Is it unbelievably gauche to return an at-home dinner invitation with a dine-out-at-a-restaurant invitation? I'd hate to subject anyone to the stuff I make myself, but I keep getting not-too-subtle pressure that I owe my friends for dinners at their house. I love eating at other people's places and, if that's the way they usually dine, that's fine with me. However, I usually dine in restaurants and I think it's only fair that we see each other in our natural environments. I'm willing to stand the tab, so why do people keep turning up their noses at the idea? Really, my home isn't that interesting. D.O.*

I'm firmly in your corner in this fight (complete with towels, sponge, astringent — and lemon wedges for garnish). And there is ample precedent for your position. In France, for example, a man's home is not only his castle, it's a fortified one at that — with the front door serving as the Maginot Line. In the best bourgeois homes, no one who cannot prove consanguinity through at least five generations or who is not a candidate for marriage is permitted to breach the threshold, much less occupy a place at table. The same holds true in Japan. All those fine restaurants and geisha houses didn't spring up in a void, you know. But short of taking up residence in the *seizième arrondissement* or the Asaka district of Tokyo where your wishes are bound to be honored by understanding neighbors, you might have to reach some sort of compromise.

In our society, breaking bread together is not enough to cement a friendship. You can safely assume your friends' primary motivation is not to be fed but to satisfy their curiosity about your living room drapes or the reading matter in your bathroom. Ye shall know them by the furniture they keep.

The next time your friends have you over for dinner, end the evening by telling them how much you enjoyed yourself and that you fully intend to return the compliment. But instead of issuing a return invitation then and there, wait a few days and send them a thank-you note. Explain that familiarity with the finer points of culinary expertise is not your strong suit, but you are eager to repay their hospitality. Suggest they come to your place for predinner drinks (which will give them plenty of time to inspect your light fixtures and find out how much you paid for your down comforter) and that you will then all proceed to one of your favorite haunts.

Stress the fact you intend to pay — repeatedly, if necessary. I suspect that they may have balked at the notion of dining out because your offer to foot the bill did not come through loud and clear. If it is in writing, there can be no misunderstanding.

DEAR EVE: *I have just come back from a holiday in the Far East. I brought back all sorts of souvenirs and small gifts for friends because I knew they would be appreciated. However, before I left one friend asked me to do him a favor. He wanted something for his girlfriend who is a whiz at the sewing machine, so he asked me to get him a special fabric. He gave me precise instructions: this color, this quality of silk brocade, so many yards, etc.*

I found it in Bangkok and brought it back as requested. The only thing is, it cost a fortune! When I gave it to him, he thanked me very much but said nothing about reimbursing me. I don't mind being generous, but I found this a bit much. How can I get him to pay me back? P.M.

No doubt the cad in question is laboring under the delusion that since you can afford such a lavish vacation, hey, what's a little silk brocade between friends? You must set him straight on this point. I hope you didn't spend too much of your time in the Orient picking up tips on how to be inscrutable.

You are right to be annoyed, but don't waste energy explaining your friend's lack of basic decency to him, especially if you still aren't fully recovered from jet lag. Instead, tell him how much the silk cost in a manner that suggests you always assumed this was a business deal. Better still, if you haven't thrown out the bill, simply present it to him (with the added thoughtfulness of having converted the bahts to dollars for his convenience). In the future, be wary of running international errands. The next thing you know, you'll be on your way to Lima and a friend will ask, "Would you mind picking up a small package for me while you're there? A guy will meet you in the lobby of the El Prado Hotel ..."

ANSWER IT, IT MIGHT BE THE PHONE

It's amazing how many people are uncomfortable with the ringing gizmo which is so central to our existence, even though it is meant to make our lives easier and comes in a score of decorator colors.

Some people (mostly women, unfortunately) spend much of their lives waiting for it to ring. The inimitable Dorothy Parker summed up that sorry state in her short story, "A Telephone Call": "Oh, please, dear God, dear, kind God, my blessed Father in Heaven — let him call before then. Ten, fifteen, twenty, twenty-five, thirty ..." Those of us who have been there would rather not be again.

Others dread its intrusion to the extent that they consider man's greatest technological achievement to be the unpluggable jack. I was once at a wedding held in a private home when the minister's pronouncement was cut short by that piercing, insistent *brrring, brrring*. The best man picked it up and was heard to bellow, "No, you may not speak to Marion. She's being married." Is there no escaping it?

There is a vague theory that a man who keeps a telephone by his bed is almost guaranteed to be impotent; the threat of a bell about to go off ("Oh, hi Mom, I was just thinking about you") ensures that his mind doesn't stay on the business at hand. Let's face it: we all loathe it for one reason or another, but it's our umbilical cord to the world around us and we wouldn't know what to do without it. I work primarily (or so it seems at times) to pay off my long distance bills.

DEAR EVE: *I have a friend who, being very wealthy, is rather cavalier when it comes to money, especially other people's. Recently, the phone rang at 6 a.m., and the operator asked me if I would accept a collect call from Switzerland. I was so groggy I said yes and found myself discussing the weather at* *home. I was boiling mad by the time I got off. Should I give her the bill when she gets back? C.K.*

Absolutely. I don't see why you should subsidize her homesickness. You weren't wrong to have accepted the call in the first place; collect calls from far off, especially at that hour, often signify trouble and if she is your friend, you should be eager to be of service. Had there been a tragedy, the cost of the call would have seemed insignificant, and something I'm sure you'd be willing to underwrite given the circumstances.

In this case, there is no reason to spare a woman of her means a sum which she might consider trifling, but one which you — and the phone company — take quite seriously. The next time she goes wandering, bid her bon voyage and urge her to send postcards.

DEAR EVE: *What do you do about friends who arrive at your house and proceed to tie up the phone, either by making calls or getting them because they gave out your number before coming? D.M.*

If one of the friends in question is a surgeon, I would sigh and ignore it. But if you mean just run-of-the-mill friends, I suggest you put your foot down and run the risk of offending them because that is precisely what they are doing to you.

People who aren't needed in an operating room at a moment's notice who behave this way are trying to let everyone around them know that they are terribly important. They treat other people's phones the way dogs treat fire hydrants — as a way of marking their passage through a territory. Try this bluff: "I would rather you didn't give out my phone number. I pay the phone company a large amount of money to keep it private. You see, I'm afraid the casino in Macao will one day trace me and force me to make good on my gambling debts."

DISCRETION IS THE BETTER PART OF SO MANY THINGS

DEAR EVE: *Like most people, I try to tell the truth as much as I can (I'm a lousy liar with a terrible memory), but lately there's been some trouble. To protect Friend A's privacy, I indulged in something close to a "little white lie." To be more precise, when Friend B asked me a question about Friend A,*

I simply shrugged, implying that I didn't know the answer. In the course of events the whole truth has come out and I have been caught. My question, more about ethics than about etiquette, is should I apologize to Friend B and explain that I was trying to guard Friend A, or just laugh the whole thing off and forget about it? P.B.

You done good, kid. The very definition of a "white lie," according to my trusty dog-eared dictionary, is a lie "uttered in the interests of tact or politeness." Better to shrug your shoulders and thereby commit a sin of omission than suggest your interlocutor *s'occupe de ses oignons*, which is French for "butt out" and rude all the same. Fibbing for a good cause is in the venerable tradition of letters to Aunt Hattie thanking her for "the marvelous combination electric can opener and clock radio. Just what we've always wanted."

Ethics have little to do with the matter — ask any career diplomat or newlywed. Jimmy Carter promised the American people he would never lie to them and look where it got him. What is at stake here is your relationship with Friend B. I think calling and explaining the whys and wherefores of your misdemeanor would be a good idea. If he has any sense at all, he should value your capacity for loyalty above any Sunday school notions of unvarnished honesty.

DEAR EVE: *The other evening, my girlfriend and I dropped by a pub, where we ran into an old friend and his date. The problem was that it was the wrong date — I mean, he is married to another woman. For all we knew, she was simply a friend or a business associate, and we were prepared to be introduced to her as such. However, our friend proceeded to become very embarrassed and set about to squirm unseemingly. We then noticed that they had been holding hands. What should we have said to convince him we could care less? J.E.*

The question isn't what you should have said but rather, what you should *not* have said. You should not have arched your eyebrows and muttered, "Well, well, what have we here?" You should have avoided all references (pointed or simply by-the-by) to his wife: no questions regarding her whereabouts, her health or anything else you might normally have brought up had you run into him nursing a beer alone. Most of all, you should not have turned to his companion and said, "You've met Jeanette, I suppose? Such a terrific lady."

If innocent conversation had failed to convince him of your discretion, you might have found an excuse to draw him aside for a moment (a well-calculated visit to the washroom, for example) to tell him point blank there was no cause for alarm. You might wish to take up your friend's philandering with him the next time you meet, if your relationship is close enough to warrant it. But that evening he was not the one to whom you owed consideration — his date was. She had done nothing wrong and should not have been made to suffer for his sins.

DEAR EVE: *A formerly close friend is throwing a bash in a couple of weeks and, although I've been to all her gatherings in the past, I'm excluded from this one. She's even gone to the trouble of telling other guests not to mention the party to me — amazing, in this day and age, when no one can be trusted to keep his or her mouth shut. Here's the problem: the co-host of this party, her boyfriend,* has *invited me to the bash, and for some perverse reason, I think I want to attend. Would it be completely uncool to show up? S.A.*

Not uncool, but aggravating beyond the call of duty and certainly beyond the bounds of pleasure. Although you are technically invited, you will hardly receive what one might consider an all-embracing welcome. It sounds as if you wish to get even with this "former friend" and, while being brazen enough to show up under the circumstances might make your point, you're hardly going to have a whale of a time. She sounds like a nasty bit of business, anyway. Go to the movies instead.

KNOCKING ON CLOSET DOORS

DEAR EVE: *I have a sex problem. Well, actually, I have a vocabulary problem. Sometimes, you find yourself discussing intimate details with relative strangers, especially when sharing close quarters. I found myself doing so one weekend at a friend's country place. I was left in the kitchen with another guest while everyone else was out doing whatever it is they do in the country.*

We started off chatting noncommittally but soon found enough common ground to feel comfortable with each other and were well on the road to friendship. He told me about his job and about good and bad times with friends and acquaintances. I told him about my ex-wife and about subsequent affairs, so it seemed only natural to push on and ask him about the women he dates. Ooops. In the midst of the question I suddenly wasn't sure if it was women he found attractive at all.

Is there some other word besides "lovers" which implies more, or "persons" which implies less, which is sexless enough to denote a question mark? T.L.

There is no other word because no other word is needed. Your almost-friend gave out enough clues to stop you when you did, and I'm sure, if you cast your mind back, certain other things he said will take on a different meaning in light of his subsequent revelation. I don't think you need worry about embarrassing him by calling things by their proper names. As one up-to-date wit put it, "The love that dared not speak its name now refuses to shut up about it."

If he felt uncomfortable at the prospect of being "found out," I'm sure he would have been sensible enough to steer the conversation on to more anodyne topics as soon as it became apparent where you were heading. I would hazard a guess, by your description of the encounter, that you were dealing with someone who is quite at ease with his sexual orientation, and who probably welcomed a chance to put his cards on the table to avoid any future misunderstanding. You were being given the option of *not* pursuing your fledgling friendship if you felt incapable of coming to terms with his homosexuality and you should have (if you pardon my choice of words) embraced the opportunity.

DEAR EVE: *Although we have never discussed the situation, I know that one of my friends is gay. We've been friends for a while now, and I really like him, but there's something really troublesome about our relationship when we're in public. In private he is very reserved, and we mostly chat about books, ideas and work. But whenever he needs a date for a professional function or for family parties, he invites me and then proceeds to shower me with physical attention. This makes me rather uncomfortable as I'm unattached and quite a few people have come to the conclusion that we're a couple. I also resent being "used." I don't want to lose his friendship. Should I confront him? G.S.*

Yes — you have every right to knock on the door of his closet. You are serving as camouflage, which is fine and dandy (and certainly part of a long-standing and time-honored tradition), but only if it is fully understood and agreed upon by both of you in advance. The problem here is that he is messing up your life in an effort not to mess up his own.

Explain to him forthrightly that you have no qualms about his orientation and are sympathetic to his need to keep it a secret, but that he's overcompensating at your expense. Urge him to go to one or two functions on his own and, if your absence is remarked upon, to explain that the two of you are just good friends. Better get the air cleared now, or ten years down the road you'll be married to him and writing to Ann Landers.

CO-VIVANTS AND CO-CONSPIRATORS

Dear Eve: *I share a house with several people. We all get along well because we've managed to lay down firm ground rules about bathroom times, phone bills, etc. But we don't "live together," i.e. eat all our meals together and socialize with the same people. I would like to have a small dinner party that I would like to keep small, and for this reason, I don't want to invite my housemates. How can I explain to them that this is a private affair? C.G.*

You can do it the subtle way, which is to leave three small steaks to defrost on the kitchen counter (as opposed to a pork roast large enough to feed the Eighth Route Army) and set three places at your dining table. Or you can do it the blatant way, which is to post "Private — Keep Out" signs on the dining room doors. Or you can do it the honest way, which is to explain to your cohabitants that you'd like to be alone with your friends.

However you choose to do it, keep the peace in the house by washing up immediately after the party so morning will not find your housemates grumbling over a sinkful of dirty dishes, "Not only are we not good enough to eat with him, I suppose he expects us to clean up after him, too."

Dear Eve: *After several months of seeing each other on a regular basis, my boyfriend and I have decided to move in together. What do you think of the idea of sending announcements out to our friends? D.Z.*

I wasn't aware that living together had achieved equal status with weddings, births and deaths. I can see it now: a Saturday morning in the not-too-distant future, over the breakfast table in a trendy townhouse. "Greg, did you know Susan and Alan are living together?" "Why? Did she call to tell you?" "No. I read it in the paper." All of which will create a torrent of letters to me asking if one should send flowers or a gift.

We aren't there yet, though we might very well soon be. Don't get me wrong: I do think the decision to live together signifies an important change in one's life, and no doubt it should be acknowledged in some way. You have several options for getting the word out as things now stand, but maybe it's time to start a new tradition.

If both of you are giving up your old places and moving into a new one, the most discreet way would be to send out change of address notices. Then all the sly devils you know can jump to the appropriate conclusion. If you are after flowers or gifts to get your little *ménage* under way, throw a housewarming party. Moving in together may be a grand occasion for you, but it's not for other people. You'll have to disguise it as something else.

Dear Eve: *Bernard and I have been living together for more than a year now. When we first announced our decision to do so, my parents objected, but finally relented. I thought we had won a victory for our generation. But my relief was short-lived when I discovered their approval was really a result of their decision to call it something else: they're telling everyone we're married. That's just not true. How do I get them to stop? L.Y.H.*

If tears and threats won't accomplish your goal, try appealing to reason, pride and greed. Point out to them that if you and Bernard ever do decide to get married, they'll have a hell of a time explaining it. The invitation list will therefore be considerably abbreviated (you couldn't possibly invite any of their friends) and the resultant wedding presents will have to be forfeited.

A FOND FAREWELL

Nothing, they say, is as inevitable as death and taxes. Just before William Saroyan died, he told an Associated Press reporter, "Everybody has got to die, but I have always believed an exception would be made in my case. Now what?"

"Now what?" isn't really a question for the dying, it's a question for the living. Some people, such as the Irish, use death as an occasion for their own marvelous brand of morose gaiety — a time when the bonds of present friendships are renewed and the memories of past friendships are celebrated. More power to them, I say.

DEAR EVE: *A close family friend of fifteen years passed away recently. I was requested to serve as a pallbearer at his funeral, a duty I accepted without a second thought. Upon opening my closet the night before the ceremony, however, an alarming realization beset me: I own no black suit. Nor, indeed, a navy blue one. The best approximation of the necessary sepulchral shade I could manage was one muddy brown two-piecer, checkered with white lines at that.*

There was not enough time to rent something more appropriate, and my difficult size requirements precluded a loan from a friend. In short, I attended in what I had (to which was added an appalling tear in the seat as I hastily jumped into a cab on my way to the funeral home).

Surprisingly, things could have been worse. There were several navy blue outfits among the forty or so people in attendance; in fact, few were in black. Some wore camel-hair or tan get-ups that bordered on the natty. Are customs for such occasions in the process of upheaval or what? Should pallbearers play it closer to the letter than others simply attending the service? S.A.

"Darkness of clothing," a member of a funeral services association informed me, "doesn't signify grief." She says you acted quite correctly. Attitudes are definitely changing, and the whole notion of enforced solemnity has been buried. Funeral directors believe that everyone attending a service should be comfortable, first and foremost. But leave your jeans in the laundry hamper where they belong; barefoot weddings may have come and gone, but I don't think we'll ever be ready for *basse couture* final farewells.

Pallbearers have neither more nor less responsibility than other mourners. The real work of lifting the coffin is carried out by the funeral home staff, and your role was primarily honorific. Some directors provide white gloves for those who will be handling the casket, but that would have been arranged ahead of time, according to the family's wishes. Obviously your friends had more important things on their minds than formality.

Most male Jews, of course, wear a head covering for any religious ceremony, and black armbands are favored by members of many ethnic groups, most notably the Chinese. Again, those may be provided if necessary. But to lay your qualms to rest once and for all, remember that the color of mourning varies from culture to culture. In India, for example, it is white.

CHAPTER FIFTEEN

How to Pass with Class

Most people, I think, would prefer to be considered travellers than tourists. Tourists never leave their home towns, except physically. Travellers, on the other hand, are eager to discover what being somewhere else is all about. You can tell a traveller by how easily he or she seeks to understand and adopt local customs. I'm not only talking about hunkering down to share some sheep's eyes in downtown Ougadougou or strutting the streets of Bombay wearing *kurta* pyjamas; one can be pegged as either a traveller or a tourist in much more prosaic circumstances closer to home. Checking into a hotel with a lover when you're not married, spending a day on a friend's boat or exhibiting *savoir faire* in a Chinese restaurant — it helps to know how to do it with style.

It's all very well to believe that when in Rome, one should do as the Romans do, but how the devil are you supposed to know what exactly it is the Romans *do* do? That's (ahem) what I'm here for. This is your big chance, you lucky people, to be privy to tips that will help you to pass with class.

Being the upwardly mobile sort, you are sure to find yourself in situations you have never encountered before. Few people grow up knowing how to behave in limousines or at a debutante ball, but now that you're on the way to a partnership in the law firm, or raking in the profits from your first film deal, you're going to have to adapt to the good life. The trick of the trade is to carrry on as though you've always lived this way. Herewith a hodge-podge of how-tos to help you tackle whatever life brings head on.

#1 Bring the Car Around, James

You're going to a dance at a swish country club. You want to arrive in high style, so you decide to rent a limousine (a Rolls Royce complete with chauffeur, if you please). But how?

Look in the Yellow Pages under "Livery." (You can also probably find it under "Automobiles, rental," but "Livery" smacks of manor houses, four-in-hands, colored silks and other accoutrements of a dearly departed decadence.) Top of the line cars go for about $20 an hour and up. If the chauffeur is required to do nothing but drive, a straight 15 to 20 percent is the customary (though not formally required) tip.

Chauffeurs have various talents, and many would be quite willing to stop at a florist's or at the liquor store on your behalf to pick up the appropriate accessories for the evening. If you make a request of this nature, increase the percentage of the tip slightly.

The principal thing to remember is that your chauffeur is a human being; he might even be studying for his doctorate in economics, so don't use the evening to indulge "Upstairs, Downstairs" fantasies. And while the main advantage of having him around is that you needn't worry about driving home yourself under the influence, that doesn't give you license to get stinking blotto. I have heard of drivers leaving passengers in such a state on the sidewalk rather than face cleaning up the resulting mess. You will earn the chauffeur's eternal respect as a lady or gentleman if you recognize the car's value and act accordingly. That means using the ashtrays, not putting your feet up on the jumpseats and refraining from carving your initials in the leather upholstery. Home, James ... and don't spare the horses.

#2 The Case of the Empty Teapot

You're in a Chinese restaurant. The jasmine tea is all gone, and the Szechuan shrimp has made you terrifically thirsty. Do you flag down the waiter and say, "Look here, my good man. May we have another round of the green stuff, please?" Nope. No way. Nosiree. If you wish to be considered Number One customer, merely put the empty teapot on the edge of the table with the lid open and pretend you couldn't care less if you ever drink tea again. It will be refilled in a flash.

#3 Unwritten Rules of the Business Lunch

No smart young man or woman on the way up aggressively orders a dry martini as soon as everyone is seated. The decision to drink at noon is one of the privileges of a senior position. If you are part of a company crowd, always defer to the senior-most person at the table no matter what your usual habits are; he or she should set the tone for the repast.

Should a waiter approach you first, his eyes agleam with the notion of the large profit to be made from an entire table of tipplers, request a ginger ale or a Perrier water if it's the sort of joint where they're likely to burst out laughing at the notion of soda pop. When it's the boss's turn, and he announces, "Yes, I'll have a double scotch on the rocks," it is quite correct to catch the waiter's attention before he goes off to fill the order and say, "I've changed my mind. I think I'll have one too."

When it's time to order food, always go with the special of the day. This communicates two important things to whomever's in charge: you don't believe in wasting time (à la carte orders often take longer to prepare) and you're not out to rip the company off by going for the most expensive item on the menu. And, just as you would never dream of ordering pizza on the first date for fear of looking less than dignified with mozzarella dangling from your lip, so too you should avoid messy food when there's business to be done. Pass up the bouillabaisse no matter how tempting it looks. It's impossible to underscore a point with one hand while wrestling with a lobster claw with the other. A sirloin, it seems, was invented with the business lunch in mind. When dining with bigwigs, forget the notion that lunch is a time to relax; you're always on duty when in the company of someone who can determine your fate.

#4 Nautical Follies

A friend who bought a boat told me he had decided it would only be fair to share the wealth. So he makes a point of inviting everyone he knows aboard as often as possible. But, he sighs, they show up in the most incredible outfits, wearing caps with braid on the visor like Marlon Brando's in *The Wild One*, and people at the marina stare incredulously.

So he has drawn up a list of guidelines for landlubbers which I feel it is my duty to share.

- No hard shoes, please. They scuff up the boat's finish and cause the wearer to skid around on deck as soon as the first wave goes by. High heels are especially hilarious.
- No pseudo high seas gear. Get the real thing or nothing at all. You aren't expected to invest in Topsiders and Brittany sweaters for just one weekend on the water; sneakers and a sweatshirt will do, unless it's one which says, "I'm the captain but my wife's the admiral."
- Don't bring cute gifts such as signs for the head which say Gulls/Buoys.
- Bring your own beer. The captain's broke from buying the boat.
- Don't expect your hosts to be galley slaves. Offer to fix lunch or bring your own.
- Speak English. A guest yelling "Keel haul the mizzenmast! Batten the bosun! Avast the mainsail!" will be deposited on dry land at the earliest possible convenience.

Well, buckle my swash.

#5 A Thumbnail Guide to Cultural Culinary No-Nos

Many people who follow strict religious or health regimes realize they place a burden on friends who invite them over for dinner, and have taken to living out their convictions so as to cause the least disruption of other people's more lackadaisical lives. Most will inform a host or hostess of any special needs when accepting an invitation with the understanding that, for example, not everyone happens to own two sets of dishes, one for meat and another for milk products. One lifelong vegetarian friend of the family has been known to arrive at our house carrying her own little casserole which needs only to be popped into the oven. She then enjoys her fair share of soup, salad and dessert along with everyone else. She adores the company and the conversation, and though it would be no problem to run up a little ratatouille on the side, she is sympathetic to the chaos in the kitchen when twelve are due for dinner at any minute. It pays to be sensitive to a guest's needs, and this little guide is designed to make you feel more at ease about getting to know people from different backgrounds.

- Ultra-orthodox Jews, as a rule wouldn't set foot in a *goyishe* household, so all you WASPs can relax about entertaining the local Hassidic rabbi. But one never knows what life will bring. If your guests are very religious, don't serve anything you didn't buy at a kosher butcher's; you'd be better off planning a "dairy" menu, one that includes eggs, cheese or any milk products. You can round out the meal with vegetables, rice or pasta, since such things are *pareve*, or neutral, and can acompany either meat or dairy dishes. Prepare everything in tin foil if you can, to avoid mixing with your usual fare. With Jewish friends who are quite religious but follow a less formal brand of the faith, you're safe with anything that doesn't include pork in any way, shape or form. (I can't vouch for those ersatz bacon bits some people inexplicably add to salads.) Shellfish is also verboten, as is any combination of milk and meat, so that cheese ravioli with meat sauce will have to wait for another occasion.

- Moslem tradition is not unlike the Jewish, but True Believers also eschew alcohol. No pig's knuckles washed down with pilsner and you're sure of not offending.
- Hindus are a varied lot since the primary tenet of Hinduism is that each individual is responsible for his or her own salvation. Salvation definitely does not include an eight-ounce sirloin or any other form of beef. Some Hindus pass up meat altogether, some eat eggs and fish but won't touch a rack of lamb, and many won't drink wine. Ask and your questions will be answered.
- Mennonites, Quakers and Baha'is will all say no to demon rum. Many also don't think a fine cigar is the perfect end to a fine meal.

You're on your own with adherents of the yin-yang way of righteousness.

#6 Christmas Without Tears

If you are the least like me, in mid-November you can't wait for Christmas (or what passes for it in the shopping malls) to be over. I'm getting to the point where I buy ear plugs in October to block out the first strains of "O Come All Ye Faithful." And one of these years I'm going to hire a hit man to get the first department store Santa who mounts a plywood throne before Halloween.

To cheer you up when this most dismal of festive occasions rolls around, and to help you avoid making Yule fools of yourselves, here are my Dos and Don'ts for the holidays:

- *Do* tip the mailman (about $5). And the building superintendent or doorman if you live in a highrise. And the boy who delivers the newspapers. If you don't consider it a token of appreciation for services rendered, think of it as a bribe for better service next year.
- *Don't* feel obliged to send a Christmas card to Snodgrass & Sons, Purveyors of Fine Plastics, or to any other business, just because

they sent you one. They deduct it from their income tax as a public relations expense. You've got better things to do with your time.

- *Don't* snap at the salesclerk just because you left all your gift shopping until the last minute. It's not the shop's fault there aren't any smalls or mediums left.
- *Do* remember the needy and less fortunate. But don't just slip a cheque into an envelope, make an effort to establish human contact — it'll help remind you what Christmas is supposed to be all about. Take some toys down to the children's hospital or buy a turkey for the nursing home up the street.
- *Don't* send yet another bottle of cheap cologne with your kids to school for their teacher. Encourage them to make something at home — a batch of cookies or a notebook covered with calico cotton. Rid the tykes of rampant consumerism any way you can.
- *Don't* give your dog a present. Resist all temptation to get Fido the electric Mr. Dentist teeth-cleaning set advertised on television.
- *Do* have plenty of hot chocolate or eggnog on hand for carolers. So what if hearing "Silent Night" one more time sets your teeth on edge? They're making an effort to spread some joy. Let them know you appreciate it.
- *Don't* send a photocopied What The Jones Family Has Been Up To letter instead of Christmas cards. I didn't even know you had an Uncle Herbie, much less care that he retired in July.
- *Do* bring an ornament if you're invited to a tree-trimming party.
- *Don't* worry about reciprocating unexpected gifts. If someone in the office hands you a pretty package and you have nothing to offer in return, don't dash out during lunch hour to even up the score. Just say, "Why, Ellen, what a pleasant surprise! Thank you" and leave it at that.
- *Do* keep all the gifts you give simple and inexpensive. A parent, spouse, lover or offspring rates something special, but don't break the bank trying to impress people with your magnanimity. If they can't afford to match it, you'll only embarrass them.
- *Don't* get drunk at the office party.
- *Do* call your mother.
- *Don't* overspend, overeat, overdrink or overdose.
- *Do* try to be merry. For everyone else's sake, if not for your own.

#7 Trysting the Night Away

Gone, thank heavens, are the days when the hotel registers of the world revealed that a significant proportion of the population was named

Smith (Mr. and Mrs.). But those days are still part of our collective consciousness — courtesy of B movie reruns on television, no doubt — and we still get nervous at the prospect of checking into a double room when our matrimonial papers are not in order.

This has never been a great problem in certain European countries, most notably France, where it has always been assumed that an important part of a hotel's function is to provide temporary shelter for illicit lovers; an arena, as it were, for the national sport of adultery. My very licit lover and I once spent an extremely uncomfortable night in the only dirty hotel in all of Switzerland where everyone from the room maid to the desk clerk kept winking at me conspiratorially.

It's doubtful that you'll encounter that sort of attitude in most places you are likely to travel to, but I strongly advise that in the few rigidly puritanical spots left in this world (Malawi is one, according to Charlotte Ford) you gracefully accept sleeping apart if the names on your passports aren't the same.

Everywhere else, to keep your affair none of the hotel's affair, follow this simple procedure: let the man do all the talking. Pipe down, all you feminists; it may not be politically correct, but it works.

If you are the male part of the equation, make reservations in your name only, specifying that you are a party of two. If you arrive without prior notice, ask for a double bed straightforwardly as though it is your business alone. By that I mean none of this "my wife and I would like" nonsense. Sign the register Mr. John Smith plain and simple, and if there's a space to fill out for number of guests, write two. Period.

If you are the female part of this equation, don't squirm when the hotel staff addresses you as Mrs. Smith during your sojourn. You'll be leaving town soon anyway; it is not worth your while to offer explanations when none are called for.

#8 Come on In, the Water's Fine

Robert Frost thought good fences made good neighbors. I think swimming pools make good neighbors. That is, I'd love it if the fellow next door put one in.

Living next door to a private watering hole presents certain temptations. Such as dropping into it every day and twice on Sunday. But if you want to make a splash in your neighborhood and still be thought a fine human being, you have to go about it very carefully.

You must realize, first and foremost, that your neighbor's pool is part of his home. You can't dip your toes into the water without his permission any more than you can wander into his living room unbidden and pour yourself a glass of his scotch. You can be pretty damn sure he knows you're dying to come over and soak your head, but there's no two ways about it: you have to wait to be invited.

Suppose your neighbor is one of those wonderful souls who believes in sharing. Suppose he knocks on your door one fine summer morning and says what you have been dying to hear. "Any time you want to go for a swim, you'd be welcome." O joy. O bliss. But hold on a second. Before you dash upstairs for your bathing suit, consider this: if he thought you were a total heathen, he wouldn't have invited you. He is assuming you understand certain principles of poolside behavior, and he's got better things to do than to stand on your doorstep and spell them all out. If he thought it necessary to take the time, here's what he would tell you:

- "Any time" does not really mean any time. Any time does not mean first thing in the morning when all the members of his household are still asleep or at the breakfast table. Any time does not mean when he has other guests there. Any time does not mean when his family is away on vacation. The pool is on his private property and, by law, he is responsible for whatever happens there. You have his permission in general, but you still need it for specific occasions.
- "You'd be welcome" does not mean all your friends would be welcome too. Arrange relay races for the gang at the local Y, not next door. Your small children may also be welcome, but they'll be even more welcome if they arrive equipped with water wings or other safety devices and if you are there to keep an eye on them. Just because he owns a pool does not mean he's qualified as a lifeguard. Your Newfoundland puppy, Screech, I can assure you will not be welcome.
- "Go for a swim" does not mean sunbathe in the nude or find out what making love underwater feels like. Unless your host advocates such activities, either verbally or by example, keep your suit on. It may be his private pool, but to you it's a public place. Go for a swim also does not mean "trek through my house dripping water." If there is a poolhouse available, use it to shower and change. If not, your own bathroom isn't too far way. You will have, of course, brought your own towels, suntan lotion and other swimming paraphernalia. And finally, go for a swim does not mean "stay for lunch." Your host may provide refreshments out of courtesy, but be prepared to cater to your hunger pangs yourself.

The fact that your neighbor has a pool and you don't does not mean you should forget to reciprocate his kindness. You must let him know you like him, not just his chlorinated playground. Have him over for dinner, lend him your lawn mower, shovel snow off his sidewalk in winter. Offer to help him vacuum the pool and clean out the filter. Or he may decide that Robert Frost was right all along and put up a fence.

#9 *White Gloves the First Time Out*

Most of you probably don't realize it, plebeian lot that you are, but debutante balls do exist. In fact, they're back with a vengeance.

Before "coming out" meant stating your sexual preference, it was a social event. When Queen Elizabeth II decided in 1958 (due either to an elevated social conscience or simply as a matter of expediency) that Buckingham Palace could no longer afford to play host to high-born maidens all dressed in white in order to inaugurate the yearly Our Crowd marriage sweepstakes, she dealt an all but fatal blow to the ritual of deb balls in the Commonwealth. Without the regal nod of approval, the custom lost its social significance and almost died out.

Then, in the mid-seventies, the balls were revived in an economically depressed England as a form of conspicuous consumption, and following the established pattern of American *arriviste* affairs became simply a matter of throwing money around.

In the United States, which had told the British monarchy to buzz off more than two hundred years before, deb balls never needed a royal excuse for existence. But during the sixties, thousands of daughters of the well-to-do refused to get out of their blue jeans for any occasion and told Daddy they planned to use the trust fund to finance a year working in the sugar cane fields in Cuba.

The balls survived in the socially conscious South, and there is evidence that they have been recently reborn all over the continent. There's the annual Trafalgar Ball in October when the *crème de la crème* of Victoria, British Columbia, dance their little hearts out aboard HMS *Discovery*. There are Polish balls in Baltimore, black balls in Atlanta, Hungarian balls in Toronto and Scottish balls in Montreal. The greatest blow-out of them all is the International Ball sponsored by the Airmen and Seamen's Club and held at the Waldorf Astoria in New York shortly after Christmas. It's a bit like a beauty pageant in that the girls represent their countries, but there are no college scholarships or modelling contracts to be won, only a look-see at who's who in international society.

You are no doubt asking yourselves, dear readers, just how you should behave if you reach the ranks where such events become a fixture on your social calendar. If you are a young woman between the ages of sixteen and twenty-four who wants to participate, you should find out which organization in your city sponsors these events and become a member in good standing. You will have to attend practice teas, learn to dance a Scottish reel or a Hungarian court dance, buy or make a long white dress, rifle your mother's drawers for a pair of elbow-length white gloves and promise Daddy you'll be good if he'll go along with the whole thing.

If you are the father of an aspiring socialite, you'll have to equip yourself with white tie and tails, foot the bill for at least one dinner at your house and buy a table at the hotel at which to seat yourself, your family and whichever of your friends you wish to impress. On the big night, you'll parade your daughter up to the dais where the guests of honor are seated, bow deeply as she curtsies, then whisk her off into the first waltz of the evening.

If you are a young man who is asked to come as an escort, you don't have to do a great deal but be attractive and couth and dance with as many young women as you can — a not unpleasurable duty. You should send flowers to the hall in your date's name, and they will be banked up in front of the head table. You may send her a corsage but check first if there are any colors or varieties of bloom preferred so you don't ruin her carefully arranged costume. Welcome to the upper crust.

INDEX